FISHING
ACTIVITY BOOK FOR KIDS

FISHING

ACTIVITY BOOK FOR KIDS

50 CREATIVE PROJECTS TO INSPIRE CURIOUS ANGLERS

DAVID LISI

Illustrated by Bindy James

ROCKRIDGE
PRESS

For general information on our other products and services or to obtain technical support, please contact our Customer Care Department within the United States at (866) 744-2665, or outside the United States at (510) 253-0500.

Rockridge Press publishes its books in a variety of electronic and print formats. Some content that appears in print may not be available in electronic books, and vice versa.

TRADEMARKS: Rockridge Press and the Rockridge Press logo are trademarks or registered trademarks of Callisto Media Inc. and/or its affiliates, in the United States and other countries, and may not be used without written permission. All other trademarks are the property of their respective owners. Rockridge Press is not associated with any product or vendor mentioned in this book.

Series Designer: Kristine Brogno
Interior and Cover Designer: Jane Archer
Art Producer: Tom Hood
Editor: Elizabeth Baird
Production Editor: Nora Milman
Production Manager: Martin Worthington

Cover and interior illustrations © Bindy James, 2021 except pp 5 (Palomar Knot), 66, 77, 97 by Monika Melnychuk; pp 59, 72 Katy Dockrill; p. 84 Kate Francis; author photograph courtesy Dominic Lisi

Paperback ISBN: 978-1-64876-892-7
    eBook ISBN: 978-1-64876-754-8
R0

I WOULD LIKE TO DEDICATE THIS BOOK
TO ALL NEW ANGLERS. MAY FISHING
BRING YOU AS MUCH JOY AND LIFELONG
PASSION AS IT'S BROUGHT ME.

CONTENTS

Welcome, ANGLERS!

I'm so glad you found this book and are starting your journey to becoming a great angler! My name is Dave, and I am a fishing guide in Alaska. I have been fishing for more than 30 years all over North America and I still can't get enough of this sport.

Just like you, I got "hooked" on fishing at a young age. It's my passion, and I spend most of my days on the rivers, lakes, and oceans chasing all kinds of fish species. Anyone who knows how to catch fish is considered an angler, and the best among us spend their lives learning as much as they can about fish and their habitats.

The activities in this book are fun ways to learn all about the ins and outs of fishing techniques and equipment. You will use these tools and activities long into your angling career. Throughout the book, be on the lookout for words in **bold**. These are technical fishing terms that you might not know, and you can look up their definitions in the back of the book. **Let's get started!**

ANGLER Ethics

Great anglers know how to find and catch fish, but they also know how to take care of the fish they catch and the places they go fishing.

Many anglers who came before us took important steps to make sure we are able to enjoy fishing as much as they did. We must do the same to make sure that the places and fish we love will thrive for future generations.

Following a personal code of angler ethics is a great way to do the right thing and protect what we love.

Angler
CODE OF ETHICS

- I will learn and practice proper catch-and-release techniques to care for fish I don't intend to keep.

- I will not keep any more fish than I need.

- I will read and follow local fishing regulations and follow the law.

- I will use **barbless hooks** to lessen damage to fish I do not intend to keep.

- I will leave the outdoors better than I found it (leave no trace, pack out what I pack in, and clean up any litter I find).

- I will be kind to other anglers I encounter while fishing.

- I will help less experienced anglers when needed.

- I will limit my impact on the outdoors by reducing noise pollution (not yelling, singing, playing loud music, etc.).

- I will try to have fun every time I go fishing, whether or not I catch a fish.

SAFETY FIRST

Fishing is a pretty safe sport. It can be enjoyed by anyone, of any age, physical abilities, or needs. There are, however, a few hazards to be aware of:

- Be careful while handling fishing hooks. They have sharp points and barbs. Always have an adult help you with fishing hooks until you get used to safely handling them on your own.

- When **casting**, be aware of what's behind you, to the left, to the right, and in front of you. Know where your hook or **lure** is at all times.

- When on the shore or wading in any water, beware of slippery rocks, drop-offs, and tripping hazards under the water. If you are fishing in a river or stream, think about the current and water depth. It's a good idea to wear a life jacket whether in a boat or fishing on the shore.

- Some fish have sharp spines and teeth. Have an adult teach you how to handle fish or keep them in a net while you remove the hook. Sharp hooks can be especially dangerous when a fish wiggles to get out of your hands or a net.

- If your hook or **weight** is snagged on the bottom of the river, don't pull up or jerk the rod sharply. This may cause the lure, weight, or hook to fly out of the water and hit you. Pull low, at hip level, until the snag is free.

You'll see safety tips throughout this book. They'll help you know what to avoid and how to stay safe while doing an activity or fishing.

WHAT'S ON MY LINE?

LURE
Artificial or "Fake" Fishing bait

SINKERS
Small devices that pull your fishing line down to a desired depth

HOOK

LINE

ROD

REEL

BAIT
Something is used to attract a fish.

FLIES

BOBBERS

SNAPS AND SWIVELS
Snaps quickly attach a lure to your line (in place of a direct tie). Can be combined with a **swivel**, a gadget used to connect two different fishing lines together.

Small floats used to suspend bait at a certain depth in the water.

Chapter 1

FISHING TACKLE

Tackle is everything you will need to catch a fish. It includes your fishing rod, reel, fishing line, and the bait or lures you use to attract fish. When you know how all of your fishing tackle works together, you will be on your way to becoming a great angler. In this chapter, you will learn:

- ☐ **The basics of fishing tackle**
- ☐ **How to understand the action of a rod or pole**
- ☐ **How to tie your line onto your reel**
- ☐ **How to find bait on your own**
- ☐ **How to make your own fly box**

LOTS O' LINE

There are many types of fishing line to choose from. Each one has benefits, depending on the kind of fishing you're doing. The weight or "lb test" of the fishing line refers to how much weight it can hold before breaking. Generally, the bigger the fish you're after, the heavier your line should be.

The most common fishing line is **monofilament**. It is pretty cheap and easy to find. "Mono," as it is often called, can be found in a wide variety of colors and is used for lots of fishing situations. It also stretches, which helps keep you from losing fish. Monofilament can break down over time with exposure to sunlight, water, and the elements—this is a good thing because it doesn't litter the water for too long. The downsides to monofilament are that it is often thicker than braid and fluorocarbon, so picky fish might see it and not bite, and it tends to float.

Fluorocarbon, or "fluoro" as it is commonly called, tends to be thinner in diameter than monofilament of the same breaking strength. Fluoro will sink, is virtually invisible in the water, and can hold up to cuts and abrasions from rocks. The downside is that it does not break down as well as monofilament. A line that breaks off in the water can remain there for a long time.

Braided fishing line, or "**braid**," is becoming more common in the fishing world. It is very popular with bass anglers because it is extremely strong and thin, and it resists abrasions and cuts quite well. The downside to braided fishing line is that it can become tangled easily. Since it's so thin, it is hard to tie and untie.

Spool of monofilament

In this activity, you will examine three types of fishing line. You can ask your local tackle shop or sporting goods store for a sample of each line. At most places, they'll give it to you for free.

Materials

A SAMPLE OF
20 LB MONOFILAMENT
FISHING LINE

A SAMPLE OF
20 LB FLUOROCARBON
FISHING LINE

A SAMPLE OF 20 LB
BRAIDED FISHING LINE

1. At your local fishing store or tackle shop, ask for a sample of each type of line.

2. Look at and feel each line. Do you notice any differences? Monofilament is usually much thicker than fluorocarbon and braided line. Braided line is the thinnest and is actually made of a "braid" of several lines woven together.

3. Try to stretch each line. Which stretches the most? Which stretches the least?

4. Try to tie some knots in each of the lines. You will notice that knots made on mono-filament tend to be the biggest knots, and knots made on braided line are very small (if you don't know how to tie knots, see Activity 2 for directions). What else do you notice about each type of line? Which one do you think would be best for your type of fishing?

RECYCLE OLD FISHING LINE

Over time, fishing line breaks down and gets old. Any time you cut line off to tie a knot or replace a section of line, it's important to recycle the old line. Most sporting goods stores, state and federal parks, and other fishing areas have locations where you can deposit old line. Never discard line in the water or on the shore, as it will pollute the water and can harm animals and fish.

KNOTS TO KNOW

Knots are the most important connection (aside from your line) between you and the fish. Weak or improperly tied knots can break or untie easily. The last thing you want is to lose the fish of a lifetime because of a bad knot! The improved clinch knot, also known as the improved salmon knot, is one of the most popular knots for anglers around the world. It's very easy to tie and really strong. It's great for tying your line to a hook, lure, swivels, weight, or flies (not the buzzing kind; the fishing kind).

Materials

FISHING LINE (20 OR 25 LB IS BEST; YOU CAN ALSO PRACTICE USING A SHOELACE OR SMALL ROPE)

A HOOK

1. Run the end of your fishing line (this end is called the **tag end**) through the hook's eye (hole), leaving about 6 or 8 inches of line.

2. Take the end and wind it around the **standing line** (main line) 5 to 7 times, leaving a loop in the line near the hook eye.

3. Run the tag end back through the loop you left at the hook eye.

4. Run the tag end through the second loop you created after step 3.

5. Pull the tag end along with the standing line and the knot will begin to tighten. *Tip: Moisten knots with water or saliva as you tighten them to prevent the line from weakening and the knot from breaking.*

6. Pull the standing line away from your hook, tightening the knot.

7. Trim your working end close to the knot. Congratulations! You've got a perfect improved clinch knot!

IMPROVED CLINCH KNOT INSTRUCTIONS

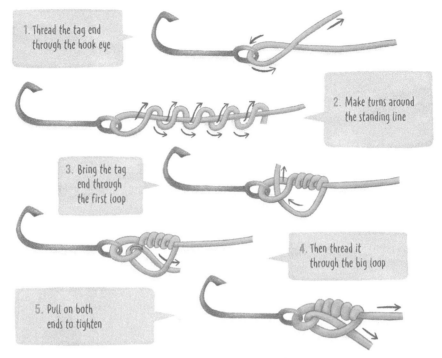

1. Thread the tag end through the hook eye

2. Make turns around the standing line

3. Bring the tag end through the first loop

4. Then thread it through the big loop

5. Pull on both ends to tighten

MORE KNOTS TO KNOW

Each of these knots can be used for many purposes, but they will work best for the specific purpose listed.

TYPE OF KNOT	ILLUSTRATION	PURPOSE
Arbor Knot		Tying your line to your reel (see Activity 6 for tying instructions)
Double Uni Knot		Tying two different lines together (see Activity 3 for tying instructions)
Palomar Knot		Tying a lure to your hook, especially useful for a drop shot rig

DIY FISHING POLE

In this activity, you'll make a simple fishing pole with a few materials you can find around the house or in your neighborhood. And yes, this pole can actually be used to catch a fish! It can also be used to practice casting (see page 68) if you use yarn instead of string and fishing line (with no hook).

Materials

A STICK (ABOUT 5 FEET LONG AND 1 TO 2 INCHES THICK)

THIN STRING, SUCH AS KITE STRING (ABOUT 2 FEET LONG)

FISHING LINE (OR YARN IF YOU JUST WANT TO PRACTICE CASTING)

A HOOK OR LURE

1. Remove any branches or leaves from the stick. A stick that starts off thicker at the bottom and narrows toward the top will work well.

2. Tightly tie the kite string to the top of your stick so it won't fall off.

3. Tie your fishing line (5 to 10 feet or more of monofilament) to the kite string, using the double uni knot or another knot of your choice.

4. Attach a hook or lure to your fishing line. That's it! You've got a fully functional fishing pole!

SAFETY TIP:
Have a grownup help with hooks until you are comfortable handling them.

DID YOU KNOW?

According to the *Guinness Book of World Records*, the world's longest fishing rod measures an incredible 73 feet 7 inches—this is longer than three female killer whales in a row! It was made by Schweizerischer Fischereiverband of Switzerland in 2011. Can it catch a fish? Probably not, but it is quite an amazing accomplishment!

DOUBLE UNI KNOT

1. Peel one end back and wrap it around both lines 3 or 4 times

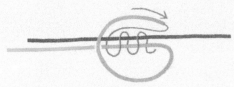

2. Pass the tag end through the loop that formed when you doubled back. Pull on the tag end to tighten. You now have one uni knot.

FIRST UNI KNOT

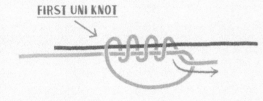

3. Make the second uni knot with the other line

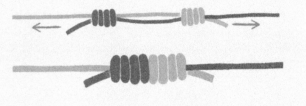

SECOND UNI KNOT

4. Pull the two standing ends in opposite direction to tighten. The two knots should slide toward each other and eventually meet.

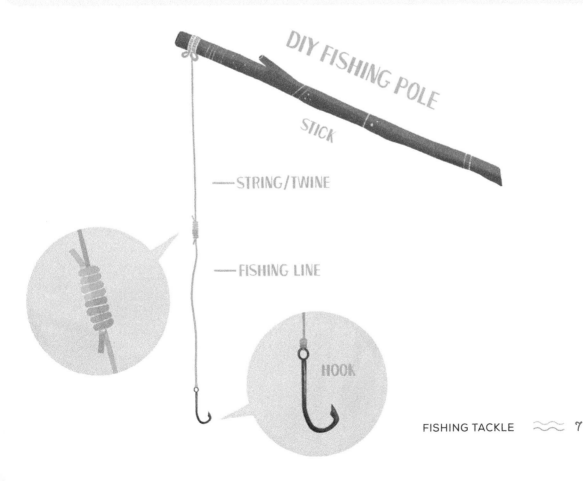

DIY FISHING POLE

STICK

STRING/TWINE

FISHING LINE

HOOK

FISHING ROD ACTION

How do you know what fishing pole to buy? Well, fishing rods (also known as poles) have different action and power, depending on the type of fishing they're used for.

The **action** of a rod means how much it bends at the tip. A fast-action rod will bend in the top third of the rod. A medium-action rod will bend in the top half of the rod. A slow-action rod will bend from the lower third of the rod. The type of action you need usually depends on the kind of lure you use. Fast-action rods are great for most times that you're fishing with bait.

The **power** of the rod refers to how much it can lift before bending. A rod's power can be ultra-light, light, medium, medium-heavy, or heavy. The level of rod power usually depends on the kind of fish you are targeting. You don't want to try to catch a giant bass with an ultra-light rod! Heavier rods are also better for heavier fishing line weights.

Materials

A VARIETY OF STICKS, ALL ABOUT THE SAME LENGTH. LOOK FOR A FEW STICKS THAT ARE RELATIVELY STIFF, SOME THAT BEND EASILY, AND SOME THAT ONLY BEND SLIGHTLY.

1. Pick up a random stick.
2. Hold the thicker end of the stick against a tabletop.
3. Bend the other end of the stick. What do you notice? Where does it bend from? How easily does it bend?
4. Repeat steps 1 to 3 for every stick.
5. Use this knowledge when you test out rods to buy. Remember that fast-action, medium-power rods are best for most bait fishing!

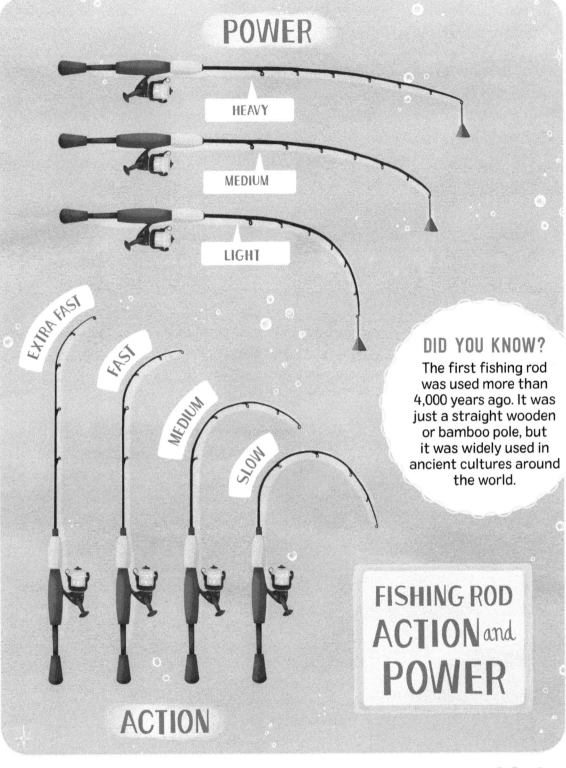

POWER

HEAVY

MEDIUM

LIGHT

EXTRA FAST

FAST

MEDIUM

SLOW

DID YOU KNOW?
The first fishing rod was used more than 4,000 years ago. It was just a straight wooden or bamboo pole, but it was widely used in ancient cultures around the world.

FISHING ROD ACTION and POWER

ACTION

REEL TO REEL

Take a field trip to your local sporting goods or tackle store to learn the basics of fishing reels and other tackle. If you can't get to a store, spending time with an angler you know is just as good, especially if they have lots of tackle to show you. There are many different types of reels, including spinning reels, baitcasting reels, and fly reels. Most reels have a spool, bail, drag, handle, and foot. Each of these parts does something important.

Materials

(Note: you don't need to buy these; just visit the sporting goods store to see them)

SPINNING REEL

FLY FISHING REEL

BAITCASTING REEL

SPINCASTING REEL

1. Choose a quiet time to visit your local sporting goods or tackle store, when the salesperson will have a moment to talk with you.

2. Look over each reel and notice the differences between them all.

3. Identify what parts are the spools, bails, handles, drags, and feet.

4. Ask the salesperson about each reel, how to cast and reel with each, and how the drags work.

5. After you've spent time handling each type of reel, ask which one would be good for the type of fishing you enjoy. The people there may also be able to give you good advice for other tackle, such as the right hooks and lures, techniques to use, and even local fishing spots.

DID YOU KNOW?

The first picture of a reel is from the painting *Angler on a Wintry Lake* by ancient Chinese artist Ma Yuan around the year 1195.

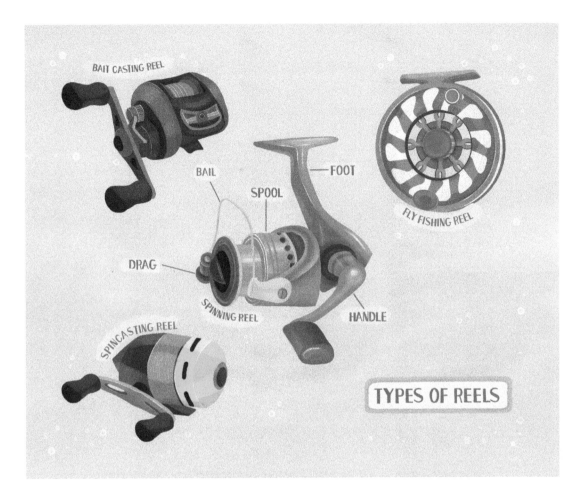

BAIT CASTING REEL

BAIL

SPOOL

FOOT

FLY FISHING REEL

DRAG

SPINNING REEL

HANDLE

SPINCASTING REEL

TYPES OF REELS

- The *spool* holds your fishing line.

- The *bail* holds the line in place and keeps it from unraveling.

- The *drag* allows a fish to pull line off the spool (this is great to have for bigger fish so they don't break your line).

- The *handle* is used to wind the spool to pull in your fishing line. It can be set up for right- or left-hand use.

- The *foot* attaches your reel to your rod.

SPOOL THE REEL

Spooling line onto your reel can be very simple. But tangles are the worst! Learn how to do it right, because if you spool the line on wrong, it can lead to lots of tangles and frustration.

Materials

FISHING LINE

FISHING ROD

FISHING REEL

ROCK OR OTHER SMALL, HEAVY ITEM

1. Thread the line through the lowest eyelet of your rod.

2. Tie your fishing line onto your reel with an arbor knot. This is the most common knot for attaching line to a reel (see instructions on the following page).

3. Place the spool of line on the floor with a rock or other small, heavy item on top of the spool (so the spool won't spin).

4. Slowly begin to reel the line so it comes off the spool in a counterclockwise direction.

5. As you reel the line in, keep it tight by pinching the line between your fingers. (Be careful! If you reel too fast, you can burn your fingers or cut them.) Continue reeling the line in until you have about an eighth of an inch of space between the line and the end of your reel spool.

DID YOU KNOW?

The earliest records show that the Chinese fished with line made of a single strand of silk. For centuries after that, people fished with lines made from animal or vegetable material, including braided horsehair!

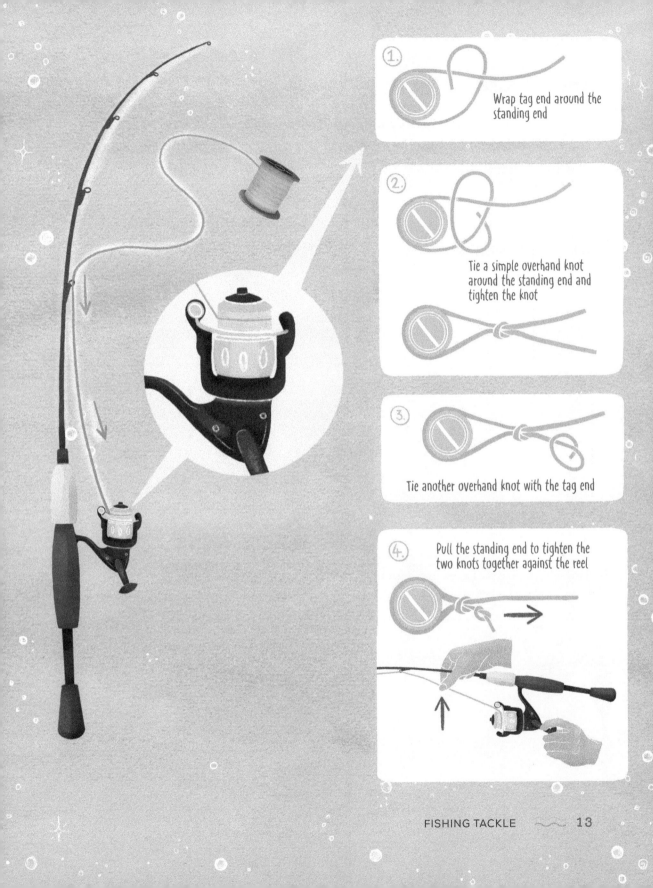

1. Wrap tag end around the standing end

2. Tie a simple overhand knot around the standing end and tighten the knot

3. Tie another overhand knot with the tag end

4. Pull the standing end to tighten the two knots together against the reel

STRING YOUR ROD

Once you have your line on your reel, it's time to learn how to "string up the rod." This will help you learn one of the most common things an angler has to deal with before fishing.

Materials

FISHING ROD AND REEL

FISHING LINE

HOOK OR LURE

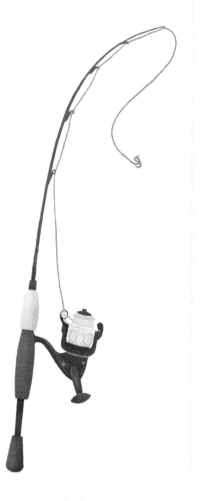

1. Pull some line off your reel. Aim to have about three to four feet of line coming off the tip of your rod.

2. Begin to run the line through the next lowest eyelet or "guide," and work your way up the rod, running it through each eyelet all the way up. Be sure not to skip an eyelet.

3. Trim any excess line. Even if you don't want to attach a hook or lure, it's important to attach something to your line to keep it outside of your rod and ready to fish.

DID YOU KNOW?

One of the most common mistakes anglers make is accidentally skipping an eyelet or guide as they string their rods. This will add friction to the line and can break your pole if you've got a bigger fish on the other end.

BACKYARD BAIT

Finding your own bait can be a lot of fun! In this activity, you will learn a cool trick for finding common bait, and learn how to catch it and store it. The most common bait for all types of freshwater fishing in North America is earthworms. These juicy treats catch lots of fish!

Materials

SMALL CONTAINER WITH A LID (A LARGE YOGURT CONTAINER OR COFFEE CAN IS GREAT)

DIRT OR SOIL

PIECE OF CARDBOARD

WATER

1. Make sure your container is clean and dry. Poke holes in the lid.

2. Gather some dirt or soil from the area where you plan on collecting the worms. Loosely fill the container two-thirds full with soil. If the soil is very dry, add a little water to make it damp.

3. Soak the cardboard in water and place it on the ground overnight.

4. Lift the cardboard in the morning, and you should see plenty of earthworms.

5. Gather the worms and place them in your container with the damp soil.

6. Cover the container and take your worms fishing!

KEEP IN MIND

Only catch what bait you think you will need for your fishing trip. It's also important to catch bait only a day or two before you go fishing. Keep your bait cool in the soil in the refrigerator. Whatever bait you have left over at the end of the day should be let go to prevent it from spoiling.

DIY FLY BOX

Fly boxes come in all shapes and sizes. They provide dry storage to protect your flies and keep them from getting rusty and crushed. These "mint tin" fly boxes are fun and fast to make. They also help reuse mint tins that normally get thrown away. The other materials used are inexpensive and easy to work with. I still have homemade fly boxes I made as a kid almost 30 years ago!

Materials

METAL MINT TIN
OR OTHER SMALL
METAL TIN

PENCIL OR PEN

4MM FOAM SHEETS
(FROM CRAFT STORE)

SCISSORS

SUPER GLUE,
5-MINUTE EPOXY,
OR HOT GLUE GUN

THIN ADHESIVE
MAGNETIC SHEET
(FROM CRAFT STORE)

SAFETY TIP:
Have a grownup
help with super
glue or hot glue,
if needed.

1. Thoroughly wash and dry your tin.

2. Trace the bottom of your tin on the foam sheet.

3. Cut the foam with scissors. Test-fit the foam to the bottom inside of your tin. If the foam is too large or needs to be trimmed, trim it to fit.

4. Spread glue in the inside bottom of your tin, and press the cut foam piece firmly into place.

5. Trace your tin on the magnetic sheet.

6. Cut the magnetic sheet to the shape. Test-fit it to the inside of the top of your tin lid, trimming if needed to fit.

7. Spread glue in the inside top of your tin, and press the cut magnetic sheet into place.

8. Once the glue has set, you can use the magnetic top for small flies like nymphs and the foam bottom for larger flies like dry flies and streamers. You can also cut the foam into small strips to create dividers in your tin, to separate different types of flies.

DID YOU KNOW?

Fly fishing is a form of fishing where the "lure" you use is often very light. Fly anglers use a thicker fly line in order to help them cast "weightless" flies at great distances. Flies are usually hand-tied on hooks using feathers, fur, and synthetic materials. Flies can imitate aquatic insects, minnows, and other prey that fish like to feed on.

DIY FLY BOX

DIY BUG NET

In this activity, you'll learn how to make your own bug net to catch bugs and learn what the fish in the area might be eating. Whether you are using live bait, lures, or even fly fishing, identifying the types of food that fish eat will help you catch lots of fish! Bug nets work really well in creeks and rivers, but they can also be used in lakes and ponds.

Materials

THIN WIRE COAT HANGER

MESH PAINT-STRAINING NET (FROM HOME IMPROVEMENT STORE)

DUCT TAPE OR OTHER WATERPROOF TAPE

1. Unwind the top of your wire coat hanger and shape the hanger into a big hoop.

2. Once you have the shape you want, twist the coat hanger together at the open end to make it sturdier and create a handle.

3. Slide the paint strainer net over your coat hanger hoop. Secure it in place with tape around the edges so the net is flat.

4. If you are in a creek or river, carefully wade in until you're at least ankle-deep in the water. Place the top of your net on the bottom of the creek or river and begin "disturbing the bottom" upstream from your net by kicking the rocks and dirt. In just a few kicks, you should dislodge lots of insects and maybe even some small fish, which will get caught in your net. Now you can see what the fish are eating, and you can make great lure or bait choices to catch more fish!

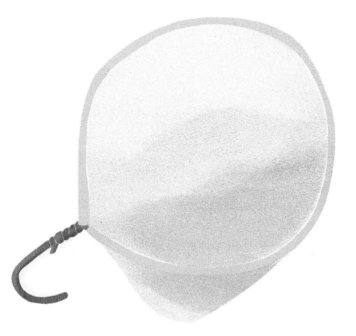

DIY BUG NET

DO I NEED A FISHING LICENSE?

When people buy fishing licenses, they help fund the protection of habitat and fish and wildlife in many states. People who purchase fishing and hunting licenses are a big part of what helps protect the outdoors. In most states, if you are 16 years or older, you will have to buy a fishing license. If you are under 16, you will not need one (just check your state's regulations and any regulations of private fishing facilities in your area). In some states, you will need special "stamps" in order to catch certain species like trout and salmon. Always check your local regulations before fishing, and obey the law.

Chapter 2

TERMINAL TACKLE

In this chapter, you will learn all about **terminal tackle**. Terminal tackle is anything attached to the end of your fishing line. Not every terminal tackle we discuss is needed for fishing, but you'll want to know what each item is as you get more experience as an angler. Each kind of terminal tackle is connected with a specific fishing style, but you can use most terminal tackle across many different fishing techniques. Let's dive right in!

In this chapter, you will learn:

- ☐ **The basics of terminal tackle**
- ☐ **How to make a leader**
- ☐ **How to make your own bobbers**
- ☐ **How to make your own hooks, sinkers, and lures**
- ☐ **How to set up a basic bobber rig**

WHAT'S IN YOUR TACKLE BOX?

Let's gather your gear for an exciting day on the water! Your tackle box is one of the most important pieces of equipment you'll have "in the field" on every fishing trip. In this case, the field is any body of water you plan on fishing—it could be a lake, stream, or even an ocean.

Tackle boxes come in all shapes and sizes. They can be made of plastic, metal, or even stiff cloth. Lately, there has been a trend toward tackle bags. These can be simple wallet-style bags with "pages" of resealable pockets, or over-the-shoulder waterproof bags with all kinds of storage compartments inside. Some tackle boxes are waterproof; others are not. No matter what, always be sure your lures, hooks, and other terminal tackle are dry when storing them after a trip. Leaving wet tackle in your box or bag can cause items to rust.

Materials

TACKLE BOX OF YOUR CHOICE

TERMINAL TACKLE OF YOUR CHOICE

1. Choose your tackle box. It can be as simple as a small plastic box you already have, or as fancy as a specially made multi-drawer metal tackle box. All you really need is a small tackle box that keeps all of your terminal tackle organized, untangled, and dry.

2. Stock your tackle box with the appropriate terminal tackle. You may want to include:

   - Hooks (choose sizes that fit the species you're fishing for)
   - **Sinkers**
   - **Swivels**
   - Lures (soft lures as well as hard lures like spinners or spoons)
   - **Bobbers** or floats
   - Extra fishing line

- Needle-nose or fishing pliers for pinching **split shot sinkers** onto your line and removing hooks from fish

- Nail clippers (No, you don't have to cut your nails! This is for helping you trim your fishing line after tying knots.)

- **Stringer** (If you're permitted to keep your fish, you will want a stringer to keep them together.)

PLIERS

SPINNER

SPLIT SHOT SINKERS

LURES

SPOON LURE

STRINGER

NAIL CLIPPERS

FISHING GEAR CHECKLIST

Along with your terminal tackle, here are some items that will come in handy in the field:

- Fishing rod or pole and reel

- First aid kit

- Sunglasses (polarized sunglasses work great for fishing)

- Hat (Wearing a hat with a brim and sunglasses will not only protect you from the sun, but this combination will also help keep you safe from flying lures, weights, and hooks as you and other nearby anglers cast.)

- Water and snacks

- Insect repellent (be sure not to get this on your lures or fishing line)

LURED IN

Making your own lures can be a pretty neat experience, especially when you catch a fish on a lure you made yourself! In this activity, you'll learn how to make a lure that catches fish with common things from around the house. This bottle cap lure is easy to make and actually catches lots of fish!

Materials

METAL BOTTLE CAP FROM A GLASS BOTTLE

NEEDLE-NOSE OR FISHING PLIERS

SPLIT SHOT SINKERS (OPTIONAL)

HAMMER

SMALL FINISHING NAIL

2 SPLIT RINGS (FROM TACKLE SHOP)

SIZE 4 OR 6 HOOK

SPLIT RING TOOL (OPTIONAL)

SAFETY TIP:
Have a grownup help with hooks until you are comfortable handling them. You may also need help with hammering.

1. Flatten the two opposite ends of your bottle cap with the pliers.

2. Place the split shot (if using) into the cap and tightly close the cap over it with your pliers. (You can also make this without a split shot, it just won't sink as well into water.)

3. Hammer a hole through each end of your cap, being careful to leave enough space at the tip of the cap.

4. Once your holes are made, carefully attach split rings to your bottle cap at each of the holes with the split ring tool/pliers (if using).

5. On one of the split rings, carefully attach your hook.

6. Congratulations, you've got a lure! You can bend the cap in half to change the action of your lure.

BOTTLE CAP LURE

1. Flatten two opposite sides of the bottle cap

2. Place your split shot sinker in the cap

3. Tightly secure with pliers

4. Hammer a hole in each end

5. Add split rings to each hole

6. Attach hook to one of the split rings

SODA

DID YOU KNOW?

One of the best lures that catches fish all over the world is the spoon—an oblong, metal lure named for its resemblance to the bowl of a spoon. The simple design seems to attract fish by reflecting light and moving like prey. These lures date all the way back to the eighth century, when Nordic people began using spoon lures made from local metals.

FOLLOW THE LEADER

In this activity, you'll learn what a fishing **leader** is and how to make one on your own. Leaders are smaller and lighter fishing lines that are tied at the end of your main line. They are important for several reasons. Because they're less visible to fish, they help anglers present lures, bait, and flies to fish without spooking them. They also ensure that you break off only small sections of line if you get a snag, or if a fish breaks off. If used with swivels, leaders can also help you avoid twists and knots in your line.

Materials

MAIN FISHING LINE FROM YOUR REEL

BARREL SWIVEL

NAIL CLIPPERS

LEADER LINE

HOOK, LURE, OR FLY

SPLIT SHOT SINKERS (OPTIONAL)

NEEDLE-NOSE OR FISHING PLIERS (OPTIONAL)

1. Tie the line from your reel onto a barrel swivel using the improved clinch knot (page 4). Trim the excess line with the nail clippers.

2. Decide how much line you will need for your leader. Most leaders are 2 to 3 feet long.

3. Tie your leader to the other end of the barrel swivel with another improved clinch knot and trim the leftover line with the nail clippers. If you don't have a barrell swivel, you can also simply tie the two lines together using a double uni knot (see page 7).

4. Tie your hook, lure, or fly to the other end of your leader line using the improved clinch knot and trim the excess. Now you've got a perfect leader!

5. Optional: Add the split shot sinker directly above the barrel swivel on your main line. Crimp the split shot on with the pliers. This will help weigh down your line into the water.

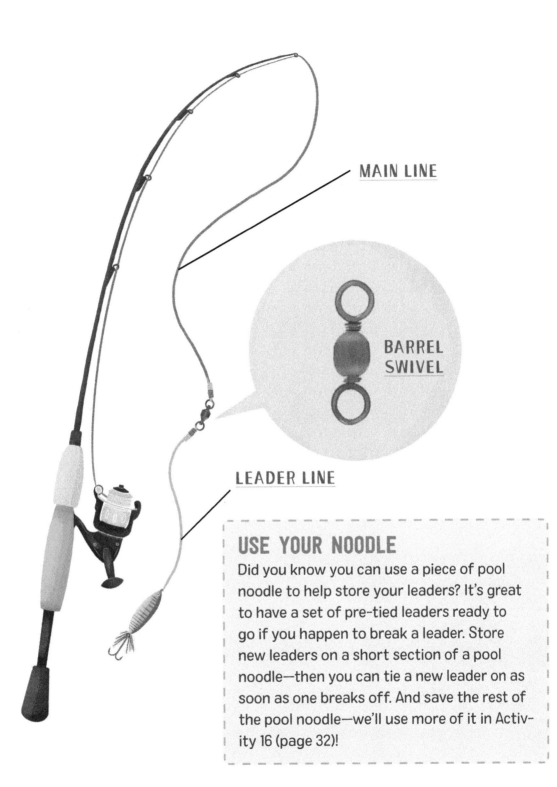

MAIN LINE

BARREL SWIVEL

LEADER LINE

USE YOUR NOODLE

Did you know you can use a piece of pool noodle to help store your leaders? It's great to have a set of pre-tied leaders ready to go if you happen to break a leader. Store new leaders on a short section of a pool noodle—then you can tie a new leader on as soon as one breaks off. And save the rest of the pool noodle—we'll use more of it in Activity 16 (page 32)!

HOOK 'EM

Hooks are the most important fishing tackle an angler will use. Choosing the right hook can be a little tricky, since there are so many different types out there. They come in a variety of shapes, sizes, and weights, can be barbed or barbless, and so on. Don't get overwhelmed—your local outdoor store, tackle shop, or fly shop is a great place to go to learn more and ask questions. Just be sure to follow local regulations and best practices for catch-and-release angling. In this activity, you'll make one of your own hooks from an empty soda can. As you can probably guess, this is a good hook to catch a bigger fish, like a largemouth bass or catfish.

Materials

SODA CAN TAB(S)

WIRE CUTTERS, TIN SNIPS, OR ANY TOOL THAT CAN CUT METAL

METAL FILE (OPTIONAL)

FISHING LINE

1. Cut a small piece from the larger loop at the top of the tab, at an angle.

2. Remove any extra metal around your cut and bend the cut loop into a hook shape.

3. Optional: Once you've removed all the metal to form a hook, you can use the metal file to sharpen the hook point.

4. Tie some line through the smaller, closed loop and you're ready to fish!

SAFETY TIP:
Have a grownup help with wire cutters and sharp metal.

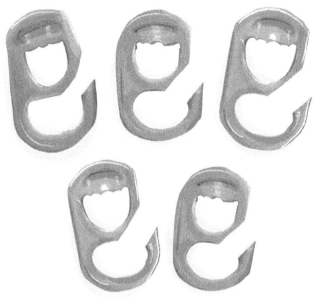

Soda tab hooks

CHOOSING THE RIGHT HOOK

Which hook should you use? Well, it depends on the species of fish you are targeting and what kind of bait you're using. If the hook is too big, it could injure a fish. If it is too small, a larger fish will not be hooked. The more you fish, the better you'll learn what works. This is also a great question to ask anglers who have had more time on the water. Check local fishing regulations—there may be rules on hooks.

CORK BOBBERS

Bobbers or floats help you position your bait at the right depth in the water. They are typically used in shallow or still bodies of water. In this activity, you'll make your own bobber from a bottle cork. Not only is this a great bobber for bait fishing, but it can also be used as a "popping cork" in saltwater fishing. Unlike freshwater fishing where "quiet is king," saltwater species are attracted to noise on the surface of the water. If you clack this cork bobber on the surface a few times, you can attract some great saltwater fish.

Materials

BOTTLE CORK

DRILL AND 4MM DRILL BIT

THIN STRAW, LIKE A COFFEE STIRRER, OR LOLLIPOP STICK

SUPER GLUE

FISHING LINE

BOBBER STOP

SAFETY TIP:
Have a grownup help with the drill and super glue, if needed.

1. Drill a hole straight through the center of the top of the cork all the way through the bottom. Test-slide the straw into the cork and use a slightly larger drill bit if the hole is too small.

2. Place glue around the middle of the straw or stick and slide it through the hole. Trim the ends of the straw, leaving about ½ inch sticking out on either side.

3. You now have a sliding bobber if you used a straw, or a regular bobber if you used a stick. If it's a sliding bobber, slide your fishing line or leader through the straw, until the bobber is 1 or 2 feet up your line (depending on how deep you want your bait to sink).

4. Tie a bobber stop above the top of the bobber to keep it from sliding too far up your line. If it's a regular bobber, tie your line to the end of the protruding stick.

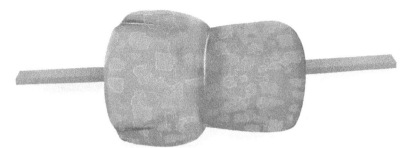

Bobber made from a cork and coffee stirrer

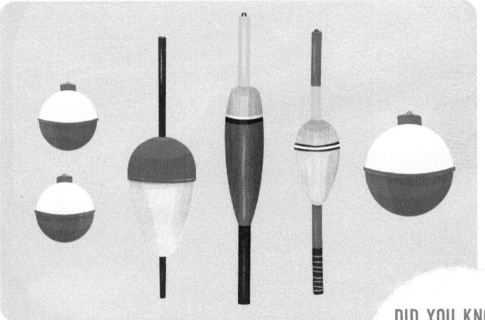

DID YOU KNOW?

Fly anglers also use bobbers/floats, but they are often called "indicators," because they indicate when a fish strikes a fly.

FLOAT ALONG

Ready to make another homemade bobber or float? This activity uses some more of a pool noodle! This time you'll use various sizes of pool noodle pieces as bobbers. Bigger bobbers (and bigger bait) are used to catch bigger fish; smaller bobbers are used for fishing smaller species.

Materials

PIECE OF POOL NOODLE

SCISSORS

THIN STRAW, LIKE A COFFEE STIRRER

SUPER GLUE

FISHING LINE

1. Cut a small section of the pool noodle. Experiment with different sizes, such as 1 inch by 1 inch, 2 inches by 2 inches, and so on.

2. Push the coffee stirrer through the top of the piece of pool noodle to create a hole. Pull the stirrer back out of the hole.

3. Apply super glue to the coffee stirrer.

4. Slide the coffee stirrer through the hole you created and leave just a little bit of the straw showing on each side.

5. Trim the ends of the straw so it slightly protrudes from each end by about half an inch.

6. Slide your new bobber onto your fishing line through the straw and tie it off.

SAFETY TIP: Have a grownup help with super glue, if needed.

DID YOU KNOW?
A lot of fish reproduce by laying eggs, but a few fish—including guppies—give birth to live babies. Great white sharks give birth to babies called pups.

POOL NOODLE BOBBER

Cut a slice of pool noodle

Cut out a rectangular shape

Insert coffee stirrer

ROCKIN' SINKERS

Sinkers or weights are usually made of heavier metals and help sink your bait, lure, or fly down to where the fish are. In this activity, you'll learn how to make your own sinkers with rocks of various sizes.

Materials

WIRE CUTTERS, TIN SNIPS, OR ANY TOOL THAT CAN CUT METAL

PAPER CLIP

NEEDLE-NOSE OR FISHING PLIERS

SOFT ROCK (PREFERABLY MADE OF SANDSTONE; YOU CAN EXPERIMENT WITH MANY DIFFERENT SIZES OF ROCKS TO SEE WHICH WORK BEST FOR CASTING AND FISHING)

DRILL WITH A MASONRY BIT

SUPER GLUE OR EPOXY RESIN

FISHING LINE

SNAP SWIVEL (OPTIONAL)

1. Open up the paper clip so that it becomes a straight line.

2. Use the pliers to bend your paper clip so that there's a small oval ring about the diameter of a pencil in the center. Trim the two pieces that extend down from the ring to about a half an inch long.

3. Drill a small hole about ¼ inch in diameter and a half inch deep into the top or side of your rock.

4. Fill the hole with super glue or epoxy resin.

5. Fit the extended piece from the oval ring into the hole and let the glue or resin dry.

6. To attach the sinker to your line, run the line through the oval ring hole and tie it off. You can also attach it to a snap swivel about 18 to 24 inches above your bait or lure.

SAFETY TIP: Have a grownup help with the wire cutters, drill, and glue, if needed.

Sinkers made from Stones

GET THE LEAD OUT

The use of lead, a metal that has been used in sinkers and weights, is being outlawed in many states. Lead can do harm to both fish and wildlife—water fowl like ducks and other birds can die if they ingest lead. This is why it's a great idea to use only lead-free sinkers when you head out on your fishing adventures—like these rock sinkers!

SPIN AROUND

Let's make one of the most popular fishing lures ever invented: the spinner blade. Spinners and spinner baits get fishes' attention with the use of metal "blades" that look like small spoons or propellers. Spinners and similar lures have caught fish for hundreds of years. Let's make our own!

Materials

MARKER

SMALL PIECE OF THIN METAL (FROM SODA CAN OR CRAFT METAL)

METAL SHEARS OR SCISSORS THAT CAN CUT THROUGH YOUR SODA CAN

SMALL NAIL

HAMMER

NEEDLE-NOSE OR FISHING PLIERS

PAPER CLIP

2 (6MM OR 8MM) PLASTIC OR METAL BEADS (FROM CRAFT STORE)

METAL FILE (OPTIONAL)

1. Use the marker to draw a figure-8 on your small piece of metal. Then with assistance from an adult, cut out the outline of the figure-8 (careful, the metal is sharp). Leave the center of the figure-8 about ½ inch wide. Smooth the edges with a metal file (optional).

2. Use your small nail and hammer to make a hole in the center of the figure-8.

3. Carefully bend a slight twist in your figure-8, twisting in the opposite direction on each end.

4. Use pliers to straighten out the paper clip. Then bend one end of the straightened paper clip into a loop. Slide one bead onto the paper clip.

5. Slide the straight end of the paper clip through the hole in the spinner blade. Slide the second bead on top of it.

6. Cut off the excess paper clip at the bottom, leaving about 1½ inches.

7. Using pliers, bend the bottom of the paper clip into a loop to match the top.

DIY SPINNER

1. Cut propeller blade from your metal or soda can

2. Hammer hole in center

3. Smooth rough edges with a file

4. Gently bend into propeller shape

5. Unfold paperclip and form a loop with pliers

6.
- Add Bead
- Add Blade
- Add Bead
- Form an eye at other end

DID YOU KNOW?

Fish have something called a "lateral line" that can sense the slightest vibrations in the water. This helps them know if their prey is injured or is distressed, making it easier to catch. One reason spinners are so effective at catching fish is that fish feel the vibrations made by the spinner blades.

SWIVELS AND SNAPS

Swivels and snaps are other common terminal tackle. Swivels can help you join two pieces of line of different weights, and they allow the lines to spin independently so there is no tangling or twisting of the line. Snaps can be used to quickly attach lures, flies, or even sinkers to your line. Sometimes snaps and swivels can be combined. This is called a "snap swivel." In this activity, you will learn how to make your own snap swivel for fishing.

Materials

SAFETY PIN

NEEDLE-NOSE OR FISHING PLIERS

BARREL SWIVEL

WIRE CUTTERS, TIN SNIPS, OR ANY TOOL THAT CAN CUT METAL

SAFETY TIP: Have a grownup help with wire cutters, if needed.

1. Carefully open the safety pin.

2. Remove the metal cap of the pin with pliers.

3. With your pliers, bend one "arm" of the pin toward you until it makes an L.

4. Slide the barrel swivel from the point side of the unbent pin arm down to the loop in the pin.

5. Grasp the bent arm with your pliers and wind the pointed end of the bent arm around the opposite arm at least two times.

6. Using wire cutters or tin snips, trim off the pointed end just after the second wrap you made with the wire.

7. Using pliers, bend the tip of the unbent arm into a small hook shape, about ⅛ inch long.

8. About ¼ inch down from the hook you made, bend the pin wire into an L.

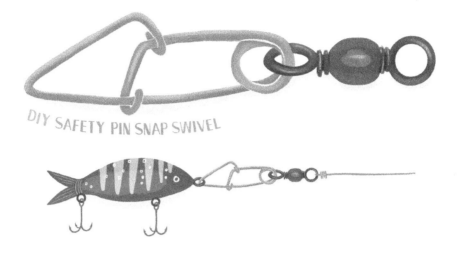

DIY SAFETY PIN SNAP SWIVEL

9 Bend the center of your pin wire toward the loop until the hook almost touches the wire near the loop.

10 With your fingers, hook the hook bend over the shank of the pin near the loop.

DID YOU KNOW?

Some fish can live up to 100 years. The orange roughy is one of those fish. Most orange roughy live in the Atlantic Ocean and Indo-Pacific Ocean.

LET'S GET RIGGY

Fishing **rigs** are basically everything you'll need on your line in order to catch a specific fish with a particular lure, bait, or fly. Some fishing rigs can be as simple as a line and a hook with bait. Other rigs can be more complicated, and include your line, a bobber or float, sinkers, a swivel, leader line, and then a hook with bait, lure, or a fly at the bottom. In this activity, you'll learn how to set up your rod or pole with a basic bobber rig for fishing with bait like worms or minnows (check your local regulations to see if bait is allowed). If you're not allowed to use bait, you can always use a small lure or even a fly.

Materials

FISHING ROD OR POLE

FISHING LINE

BARREL SWIVEL

1 OR 2 SPLIT SHOT SINKERS (3/0 SIZE WORKS GREAT)

NEEDLE-NOSE OR FISHING PLIERS

LEADER LINE (LIGHTER THAN YOUR MAIN FISHING LINE)

HOOK, LURE, OR FLY

BOBBER OR FLOAT

BAIT (IF ALLOWED)

1. String your rod with fishing line from your reel, being sure to pass the line through every eyelet of your rod.

2. Attach a bobber or float 4 to 6 feet above the end of your main fishing line.

3. Tie a barrel swivel on to your main fishing line using an improved clinch knot (page 4).

4. Above the barrel swivel, pinch 1 or 2 sinkers onto your line with pliers.

5. Attach 2 to 3 feet of leader line or lighter fishing line to the other end of your barrel swivel.

6. Tie a hook, lure, or fly onto the end of your leader.

7. Add the bait to the hook, if using.

BOBBER RIG

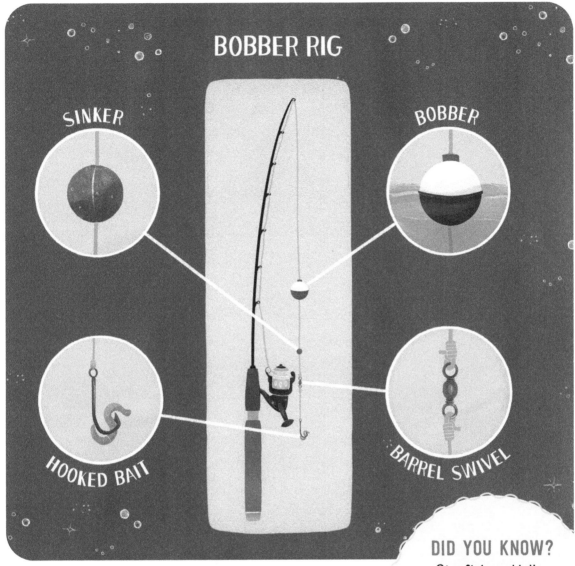

SINKER

BOBBER

HOOKED BAIT

BARREL SWIVEL

DID YOU KNOW?

Starfish and jelly-fish aren't really fish. Though not the same type, starfish and jelly-fish are both part of a group of invertebrate marine animals.

Chapter 3

FIND THE BEST FISHING SPOTS

Learning how to find the spots where fish are most likely to be is a skill that anglers spend a lifetime trying to perfect. They say that 10 percent of anglers catch 90 percent of the fish, and sometimes that feels true! Those 10 percent focus on studying the signs around them to predict where fish are likely to be. Let's learn how to "read" water and nature to find fish in freshwater areas like lakes, ponds, reservoirs, rivers, and streams.

In this chapter, you will learn:

- ☐ **How to test water clarity (clearness)**
- ☐ **What water temperature and currents can tell us about where fish are**
- ☐ **What a fish ladder and watershed are**
- ☐ **How the wind and moon affect fish behavior**
- ☐ **How to draw your own fishing map**

CLARITY TESTER

Water clarity can affect fish behavior. Though some fish live in rather silty (silt is a dusty sediment) water like the Kenai River, a glacial river in Alaska, many fish have to adapt to higher or lower amounts of sediment in the water. They will still feed (eat) when the water is "cloudy," but they may have more trouble seeing your lure, bait, or fly.

This activity is all about measuring the clarity of water. It's pretty easy and it'll help you the next time you go fishing. When you can't see the white anymore, you can make a note of it on your string and get a good idea of the clarity of the water. If there's too much sediment in the water and the white disappears right away, fish might not be able to see your lure!

Materials

AN OLD RECORD (YOU CAN OFTEN FIND THESE AT SECONDHAND AND THRIFT STORES)

WHITE DUCT TAPE OR OTHER WATERPROOF TAPE

A LONG SECTION OF PARACORD OR ROPE

SOMETHING TO TIE ON THE ROPE THAT WILL HELP THE RECORD SINK, LIKE A ROCK

1. Tape a large X on your record.

2. Fill in two opposite quarters of the record with white duct tape. You should see one-quarter white, one-quarter black, one-quarter white, and finally one-quarter black again (see the picture on page 45).

3. Tie a knot around a rock and run the rope through the bottom of the record opposite of the side you taped.

4. Tie a knot on the taped side right where the rope exits the hole.

5. Tie knots every 4 inches from the bottom up about 40 inches or so, leaving plenty of rope after your last knot.

6. Lower the rope with the record into the water at your favorite fishing spots. See how clear the black and white colors are in different waters, and how deep you can go and still see the colors.

DID YOU KNOW?

Most fish cannot swim backward. That's mostly due to how they absorb oxygen through their lungs. The water has to pass through their mouths, over their gills, and out their gill plates. It's hard for fish to absorb water going in the opposite direction.

WATER CLARITY TESTER

ROPE—

OLD RECORD

GO WITH THE FLOW

Fish are creatures of habit and have favorite hangouts along streams and rivers. Current seams, which are the places where fast and slow water meet, are excellent places to find fish. You can also find fish in areas where the surface current is at "walking speed," meaning the current is moving at about the same pace as you can walk.

In this activity, you'll see currents form before your eyes! This project mimics how currents form in oceans and even lakes and can help you identify currents on the water.

Materials

CLEAR OR WHITE BAKING DISH

COLD WATER

BLUE AND RED FOOD COLORING

1 OR 2 CUPS ICE

4 CUPS WATER (FOR BOILING)

SAFETY TIP: Hot water can cause serious burns. Have a grownup help with boiling and pouring the hot water.

1. Fill the baking dish about one-third full with cold water.

2. Add a few drops of blue food coloring to the cold water (don't add too much; you don't want the water to be too dark).

3. Add the ice and stir. Let the ice melt a little bit so the water is ice cold.

4. While the ice is melting in the blue water, boil the 4 additional cups of water with a grownup and add several drops of red food coloring to it once it is boiling. Make this water darker.

5. Pour some of the red boiling water into a corner of the baking dish with the blue water and observe what happens.

6. The hot water will push through the cold water, creating currents. Eventually, the water will mix and make purple lukewarm water, much like what happens in the ocean and in ponds, lakes, and reservoirs.

OCEAN CURRENTS EXPERIMENT

RED WATER

BLUE WATER

BEWARE OF WATER HAZARDS

Rivers and streams are great for fishing, but they can also be dangerous with their swift currents, slippery rocks, and tripping hazards such as logs and other debris. Always be careful when wading in streams and rivers. Flowing water can sweep you downstream quickly. Be sure to have an adult nearby whenever you are wading in moving water. It is also a good idea to wear a life jacket and use a wading staff (stick) in rivers and streams for balance.

WHAT'S A WATERSHED?

Through gravity, all the rain, snow, and ice eventually flow across the land to form what is called a watershed. A watershed usually refers to a geographical area where water drains over some distance into increasingly larger bodies of water. Everything from a drop of water running down a rock to tiny trickles of water through the mud or grass eventually ends up in a bigger body of water.

It's important to know how watersheds work because water from hundreds or even thousands of miles away can eventually fill up the stream, river, reservoir, pond, lake, or ocean you are fishing in. Even the tiniest amount of water matters, especially if it's carrying pollution.

In this activity, you will build your own watershed to see how water moves. Let's get into it!

Materials

A LARGE TRAY, WATERPROOF SURFACE, OR OUTSIDE PICNIC TABLE THAT CAN GET WET

RANDOM OBJECTS LIKE SMALL BUCKETS, PLASTIC CONTAINERS, TOWELS, ETC.

CLEAR OR LIGHT-COLORED TRASH BAG

CLEAN SPRAY BOTTLE FILLED WITH WATER

FOOD COLORING (OPTIONAL)

DIRT (OPTIONAL)

1. Begin by building a random landscape on top of a tray, waterproof surface, or outside picnic table with the objects you've collected.

2. Cover your landscape with a plastic bag and press down gently to form hills, mountains, valleys, and canyons.

3. Spray water at the tops and sides of the mountains to simulate rainfall or snow melt.

4. Observe as the water forms small streams, rivers, and lakes and runs off the landscape to "the ocean."

5. BONUS: Add a drop of food coloring or even a little dirt at random spots and watch how the water will carry everything throughout the system—this mimics things like pollution and mud.

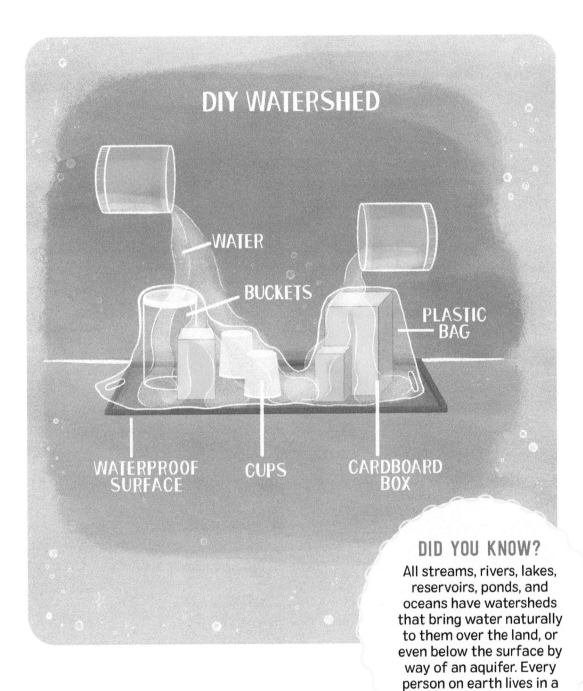

DIY WATERSHED

WATER

BUCKETS

PLASTIC BAG

WATERPROOF SURFACE

CUPS

CARDBOARD BOX

DID YOU KNOW?

All streams, rivers, lakes, reservoirs, ponds, and oceans have watersheds that bring water naturally to them over the land, or even below the surface by way of an aquifer. Every person on earth lives in a watershed of some kind.

SUPER STRUCTURE

Structure is vital for fish survival. Fish use structures to keep safe from predators, ambush their prey, and rest when they are not feeding. Structure can be a rock, submerged tree limb, overhanging riverbank, underwater roots from a nearby tree in the water, deep ledge, or even the waves created by flowing water over a fish in a stream or river. Learning to identify where structures might be underwater is important, because they're usually great places to find fish! This activity is all about making your own structure or fish attractor. What other creative ideas do you have for fish structure? You don't need a lot of water to do this—you can even make a structure in a small stream with a handful of branches and rocks.

Note: Make sure you have permission before building any underwater structure on property that does not belong to you.

Materials

OLD (REAL) CHRISTMAS TREE OR DISCARDED BRUSH

TREE LIMBS

ROCKS

STREAM OR SMALL BODY OF WATER

1. Arrange your items (old Christmas tree, discarded brush, tree limbs, and/or rocks) under the water into an attractive habitat for fish.

2. Include lots of places for fish to hide (this includes overhanging limbs, "caves," etc.).

3. Be creative and build an awesome habitat for fish and see what kinds of fish call it home!

FISH OBSTACLES

Many fish species migrate. Some, like Pacific salmon, migrate hundreds or even thousands of miles from the ocean up streams and rivers to breed. Their young spend a year or two in these freshwater streams and rivers before they migrate out to the ocean to live their adult lives. When fish migrate, obstacles can get in their way. Everything from a small waterfall to a steep run (an underwater hill), big rocks, trees, and even man-made dams get in their way. In this activity, you can go to a local stream or river and see natural and man-made obstacles that fish must overcome in order to migrate. What obstacles can you observe?

Materials

A LOCAL CREEK OR RIVER

A NOTEPAD AND PEN/PENCIL

1. Visit a local stream or river in your area.

2. Observe areas where fish might have a hard time passing—this could be a waterfall, rocks, shallow water, a dam, etc.

3. Write down what you observe and try to map out the route fish might take to overcome these obstacles. Will they swim around the rocks, jump the waterfalls, or is there another way around? Mapping out these routes can help you figure out where you might find groups of migrating fish!

FISH LADDERS

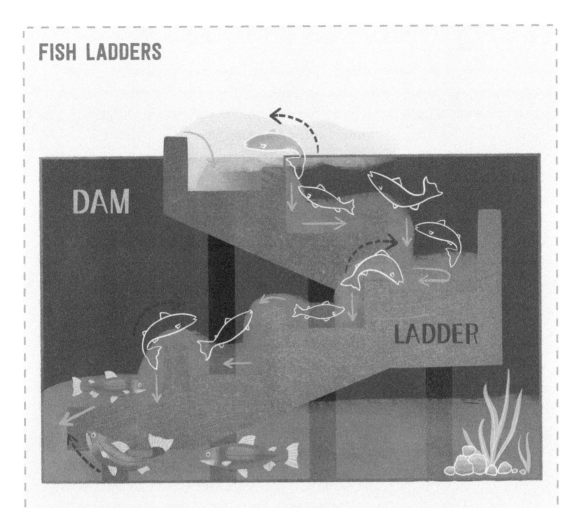

Many fish make "migration runs," where they will relocate to find food or places to mate. Sometimes they'll encounter dams or other obstacles on the way. Man-made structures known as fish ladders can help fish pass through these obstructions. A fish ladder is a series of cascading pools of rushing water. Fish leap into one pool, rest as needed, then leap into the next until they are in the next body of water.

TESTING TEMPERATURES

Almost all fish are cold-blooded. This means they can't keep their body temperature at a constant level. As temperatures rise, so do their body temperature and activity level, which can also result in better fishing opportunities. In most cases, as temperatures get colder, fish become less active, so the fishing may be poorer. When temperatures remain consistent (the same), the fish remain consistent, and you can predict where they will be and how they are biting.

In this activity, you'll learn how to use a water thermometer. Knowing the water temperature from one fishing trip to the next will help you understand how the fish may behave.

Materials

SINKING POOL THERMOMETER

ROD AND REEL WITH STRONG FISHING LINE

1. Tie a pool thermometer with an improved clinch knot (page 4) to your fishing line on your rod and reel.

2. Drop your pool thermometer off a dock or boat, or in a slower/deeper part of a river or stream.

3. Check the temperature at various depths by keeping the thermometer at the depth for several minutes. Notice any temperature differences between depths.

SAFETY TIP:
Always wear a life jacket when fishing from a boat or near deep water.

WHERE TO FIND FISH SPECIES
BY WATER TEMPERATURE

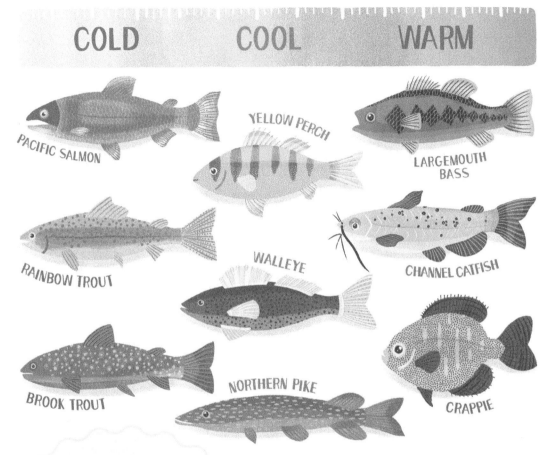

COLD   COOL   WARM

PACIFIC SALMON

YELLOW PERCH

LARGEMOUTH BASS

RAINBOW TROUT

WALLEYE

CHANNEL CATFISH

BROOK TROUT

NORTHERN PIKE

CRAPPIE

DID YOU KNOW?

Not all fish are cold-blooded. In 2015, researchers discovered that the opah, a fish that can live in water as deep as 1,300 feet below the surface, is actually warm-blooded. Though the opah's blood is not as warm as other warm-blooded animals', the warm blood that circulates through their body gives them a tremendous advantage in the cold water. It allows them to hunt and chase down prey. They circulate warm blood by constantly flapping their fins.

WHERE THE WIND BLOWS

Wind plays an interesting role in fish behavior. Wind can blow food to and from different areas in a body of water so fish can access it. Knowing where the wind might be pushing food can help anglers locate fish to catch.

In this activity, you will make a windsock to learn all about wind and see what direction the wind is blowing. Let's get started!

Materials

CONSTRUCTION PAPER

MARKERS, STICKERS, AND/OR CRAYONS (OPTIONAL)

STAPLER OR MASKING TAPE

SCISSORS OR HOLE PUNCHER

CURLING RIBBON, YARN, OR STRING

1. Optional: Decorate the construction paper using markers, stickers, and/or crayons.

2. Bend the construction paper into a cylinder and staple or tape the ends together.

3. Cut or punch two holes at opposite sides of one end of the cylinder.

4. Thread the ribbon through the holes and tie it together with enough slack to hang it.

5. Optional: Cut or punch holes at the bottom of the windsock and tie curling ribbon to the holes, allowing the ribbon to hang down.

6. Hang your windsock and see which way the wind is blowing.

PAPER WINDSOCKS

DID YOU KNOW?

Most fish don't have eyelids. Some sharks do, but it is mainly to protect their eyes as they devour their prey. Since they don't have eyelids, fish can be a little shy when it is very bright outside. This is why most anglers have success in the early morning and evenings, when the sun is not shining overhead. See if this timing helps with your angling success.

LEARN LUNAR CYCLES

Did you know that the moon can play a major role in fish behavior? Understanding the lunar (moon) cycles can greatly increase your chance of catching fish.

The lunar cycles really affect ocean fishing and river fisheries that depend on the tides. The idea is that the bigger the tide, the more active the fish. The strongest tides happen twice a month: during a new moon, when the sun and moon are both pulling in the same direction (and you can't see the moon), and the full moon, when they're pulling on either side of the planet.

Materials

FISHING JOURNAL
OR NOTEBOOK

1. In your fishing journal (see Activity 40), record your catches, and even record when you don't catch fish, during the new moon and full moon phases (this may take several months).

2. Try to fish more than one time during the full moon and new moon. Do you notice anything about your success rate during these moon phases? Were there other things that might have helped or hurt your success (bait or lure used, weather, location)?

WAXING GIBBOUS

FIRST QUARTER

WAXING CRESCENT

NEW MOON

FULL MOON

WANING GIBBOUS

LAST QUARTER

WANING CRESCENT

DID YOU KNOW?

The moon phase can have a dramatic effect on tides. The largest tides in the United States are located near Anchorage, Alaska, in Cook Inlet. The water level can rise up to 40 feet during high tide. That's a lot of water!

BAROMETRIC FISHING METER

Barometric pressure is the measurement of air pressure in the atmosphere. As the barometric pressure increases or decreases, it affects the swim bladder of a fish, which is what helps a fish stay stable in the water, especially in shallow water. Quick drops in barometric pressure can make fishing great—so can a barometric pressure that stays the same. But when the barometric pressure rises quickly, the fishing may not be as good.

Materials

GLASS JAR

NEW, UNINFLATED BALLOON

SCISSORS

SEVERAL RUBBER BANDS

SMALL PIECE OF THICK PAPER LIKE CARDBOARD, PREFERABLY A BRIGHT COLOR

2 PLASTIC DRINKING STRAWS

SUPER GLUE

ADHESIVE TAPE

RULER

1. Set the glass jar on a flat surface.

2. Cut off the rolled (open) end of the balloon and keep the other end (the round part).

3. Stretch the balloon so it tightly seals the mouth of the jar, with no leaks or looseness.

4. Stretch the rubber bands over the mouth of the jar to keep the balloon firmly in place and airtight.

5. Cut out a shape of a small arrowhead from the cardboard, with a pointy tip. Insert the arrowhead into one end of the straw. If it's wobbly and not staying in place, try making another arrowhead that's a bit wider. If it's too large, trim the arrowhead's base until it fits snugly in the straw tip.

6. Insert the second drinking straw into the empty end of the straw with the arrowhead, so they become a long, stable straw.

7. Place a bit of super glue onto the center of the balloon jar covering. Place the empty end of the long plastic drinking straw on

the glue. Gently secure it in place with light pressure and then tape it down until the straw is secure.

8 Tape the ruler to a wall. Set the barometer next to it and arrange the arrowhead to point to ruler markings. Track the number on the ruler daily to see if the barometer has risen, dropped, or remained the same. This works because at the time you sealed your jar, you trapped air inside it that was the exact same pressure as the air on the outside of the jar. But as barometric pressure rises and drops, it changes the amount of air pressure applied to the balloon outside the jar. Pretty cool, huh?

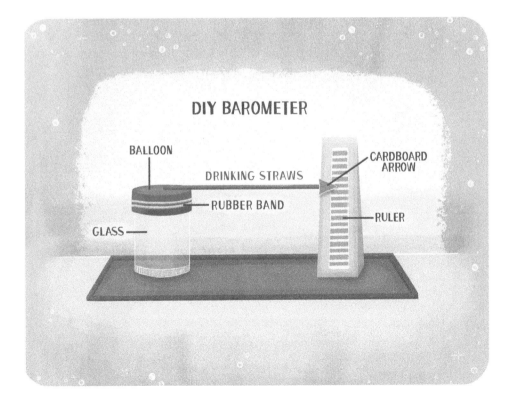

DIY BAROMETER

BALLOON
DRINKING STRAWS
RUBBER BAND
GLASS
CARDBOARD ARROW
RULER

DIY FISHING MAP

This is a great activity to help you notice the features of the water you like to fish in. Head out to a local river, stream, lake, pond, reservoir, or other body of water. Observe what you see and map it out.

Materials

MAP

NOTEBOOK OR
SKETCH PAD

PENCIL OR PEN

1. Head out to your favorite fishing spot or to some nearby water.

2. Look around and notice things such as the shoreline, a bend in a river or stream, rocks and trees in the water, eddies (circular currents), and other structures.

3. Based on what you learned in this chapter, where do you think the fish will most likely hang out? Mark some of those spots on your map.

4. Draw what you see, and draw some fish where you think they are (or where you catch some!).

FISHING MAP

LEGEND

- ⬤ DEEP WATER
- ⬤ SHALLOW WATER
- BEACH
- LARGE ROCKS
- DOCK
- --→ STREAM BEND
- ≡≡≡ STRONG CURRENT
- WATERFALL
- CHANNEL CATFISH
- LARGEMOUTH BASS

Chapter 4

FISHING TECHNIQUES

In this chapter, you'll put your knowledge to the test by learning techniques to catch fish. There are lots of different fishing techniques around the world. We'll explore some of the most common fishing techniques that seem to catch fish, such as:

☐ How to properly bait your hook

☐ How to cast

☐ How to "troll" for fish

☐ How to make your own fish trap

☐ How to properly handle the fish you catch, to prevent injury to yourself or them

HOW TO BAIT A HOOK

It's no surprise: The longer you fish, or the longer your bait is in the water, the greater your odds are of catching a fish. In this activity, you'll learn how to bait a hook with natural or artificial bait so that it stays securely on your hook for as long as possible. Use an improved clinch knot (page 4) to tie on your hook, lure, or fly.

Materials

FISHING HOOK

LIVE EARTHWORMS
OR NIGHT CRAWLERS

SAFETY TIP:
Be very careful while hooking the worm.

1. Stick the point of the hook all the way through the worm, about ½ inch from the end of the worm.

2. Push the worm to the top of the hook.

3. Grab the long end of the worm and push the hook point through the worm again, about ½ inch down from the first spot.

4. Repeat this several times until there is about ½ inch of worm left.

5. With your worm on your hook, cast into an area where you think fish are, and hold on!

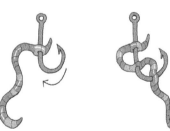

KNOW WHERE YOUR HOOK IS

Avoid injuries by always being aware where the hook point and the barb of the hook are. If you're new to working with fishing hooks and casting, have an adult or experienced angler help you out.

SET THE DRAG

Most fishing reels have a mechanism that adjusts the **drag**, the pair of friction plates on your reel that controls the amount of line you let out. This allows a fish to run and take line when it needs to; it also ensures that when a fish goes on a run, it won't break the line or come off due to too much tension.

ADJUST THE DRAG OF YOUR REEL

In this activity, you will learn about drag systems on common spinning reels. The more you fish on various drag settings, the more you'll get a good "feel" for what the proper drag setting should be for different situations. Everyone makes mistakes with drag at first, but the more you fish and practice, the better you'll get.

Materials

ROD SPINNING
REEL WITH LINE

1. Tie your line to your reel and string up your rod (see Activities 6 and 7). Pull on the line so it comes off the reel.

2. If the drag feels too light, tighten it by turning the dial to the right (clockwise).

3. If the drag feels too tight, loosen it by turning the dial to the left (counterclockwise).

4. Test out different drag settings as you fish.

CASTING PRACTICE

Learning how to properly cast a rod will help you cast farther and more easily. Casting is something that takes a little practice (you can even practice in your backyard—see the next activity). It's helpful to practice with an experienced angler who can help walk you through the steps.

Materials

SPINNING ROD
AND REEL

LURE ON ROD

SAFETY TIP:
Always know where your lure or hook is, especially as you cast.

1. Hold the handle of the rod naturally in your dominant hand with the rod positioned about mid-waist, and the spinning reel positioned below the rod.

2. Line up the bail of the spinning reel with the rod. (The bail is what holds the line on the reel.) Reel in your line so that there's about 6–12 inches hanging from the tip.

3. Grab the line with your index (pointer) finger.

4. With your free hand, open the bail by flipping it up, while keeping your finger against the line on the rod to keep it from coming off the reel.

5. Look to the spot where you want to cast (this is where your rod tip should end after your cast).

6. Raise your rod overhead and slightly behind you (know where your hook or lure is at all times).

7. Begin to move the rod forward in a casting motion and add some power.

8. Release your index finger from the line and stop your rod once it's pointed at your target (your arm should be at a 45 degree angle).

9 Allow the weight of your lure to pull the line from your reel. The cast should be one fluid motion.

10 Close the bail of your reel—you're fishing!

1. Hold the rod in your dominant hand with the reel below the rod.

2. Reel in your line so that there's about 6–12 inches hanging from the tip.

3. Grab the line with your index (pointer) finger.

4. With your free hand, flip the bail up while keeping your finger on the line.

5. Raise your rod overhead and slightly behind you, then bring it forward, releasing the line with your forefinger with your arm is around 45 degrees.

6. Close the Bail

BACKYARD FISHING

Now that you've learned how to properly cast, it's time to practice! You can use your backyard or any other outdoor space. You can even set up targets and other objects around your yard to help you become a better caster and angler.

Materials

ROD, REEL, AND FISHING LINE

PRACTICE CASTING PLUG (FROM SPORTING GOODS SHOP OR ONLINE)

OBJECTS SUCH AS HULA-HOOPS, CARDBOARD BOXES, AND BUCKETS FOR TARGETS

1. Tie your practice casting plug to the end of your fishing line using an improved clinch knot (page 4).

2. Set up your objects at various distances and angles from where you will be standing.

3. Start by trying to hit or land your plug on the objects closest to you and work your way out.

4. Give yourself points for hitting different targets (smaller and farther targets are worth more points).

5. Try to beat your high score every time you practice.

6. Make it interesting by challenging your angling and non-angling friends!

DID YOU KNOW?

Steve Rajeff of the United States holds the world record for the longest cast using a one-handed fly rod. The cast was 243 feet long—about the distance across the Mississippi River at Lake Itasca, Minnesota!

TROLLING FOR FISH

Trolling is a very effective way to catch fish. Most often, trolling is done with a boat, but you can practice without one (and you might even catch a fish!). Let's try to do a bit of trolling, shall we? I'll show you how.

Materials

FISHING ROD, REEL, AND LINE

HOOK WITH BAIT, LURE, OR FLY

1. Head out to your favorite fishing spot.
2. Cast your bait, lure, or fly out into the water.
3. Begin to walk along the shoreline at the pace you would normally retrieve a lure or bait (you may need to speed up your pace or slow down).
4. Try to keep your lure, bait, or fly moving at a consistent speed.
5. Try walking a few times. Did you catch any fish? It may take several tries, but you just might catch a fish using this method.

DID YOU KNOW?

A jig is a popular fishing lure used around the world. Jigs are hooks with heavier weights toward the eye of the hooks. Usually, jigs have materials tied to them like feathers. The action of the heavier head on the hook gives lures a jerky, unpredictable action, often referred to as "jigging." Fish are attracted to these jerky motions since many of their prey move this way, especially when injured. Give jigs a try and see how many fish you can catch!

IT'S A TRAP!

Fish traps are popular for trapping smaller bait fish that larger fish like to feed on. Smaller live fish that you catch in a trap make great bait. Be sure that using fish traps and live bait is legal in your favorite home waters. If bait is not legal, you can always use a lure or fly to imitate smaller bait fish. Let's make a fish trap!

Materials

PLASTIC SODA BOTTLE

KNIFE OR SCISSORS

SMALL ROCKS

BAIT (WORMS OR OTHER SCENT)

1. Carefully cut off the top one-third of the bottle. Keep both parts.

2. Place the bottle on its side. Place a couple of rocks on the bottom of the bottle (enough to hold the bottle on the bottom of the water). Place the bait on top of the rocks.

3. Remove the bottle cap.

4. Flip the top of the bottle upside down and insert it into the other end of the bottle until it's snug and cannot back out.

5. Place your fish trap on its side under the water and wait for a fish to swim in for the bait! You can also attach a rope to your trap and suspend it from a low-hanging branch over the water (make sure that it's fully submerged under water or it won't work!).

SAFETY TIP:
Have a grownup help with or supervise cutting the bottle.

SAFE FISH HANDLING

It is important to handle fish safely for two reasons: 1) so you don't get injured and 2) so you don't injure them (especially if you don't intend to keep them).

Some fish have sharp teeth, fins, and even small spikes on their gill plates. These help fish protect themselves against predators. The best way to practice safe fish handling is learning all about the fish species you intend to fish for. Let's take a largemouth bass, for instance. They have spikes or "spines" on their dorsal fins (on their back) that can prick you, along with sharp gill plates. This activity will have you practice proper handling techniques using a wet towel so you'll be prepared to use them while fishing.

Materials

SINK, BATHTUB, OR LARGE CONTAINER

WATER

HAND TOWEL

1. Fill the sink, bathtub, or container with water.

2. Soak the hand towel under the water. Wet your hands, too.

3. Pull the hand towel out of the water as if it is a fish (support the towel so it's parallel to the ground). Hold it firmly without squeezing too hard.

4. Hold your breath while the towel is out of the water to help you understand that fish cannot breathe when they are out of the water.

5. Repeat these steps until you feel like you can gently and safely hold a fish that has sharp parts.

CAPTAIN HOOK

By now, you know that hooks are sharp and can be dangerous if handled incorrectly. At some point in your fishing career, you may end up with a hook stuck in your skin. This happens with casting accidents, knot-tying accidents, or even from stepping on a hook.

This activity will help you learn how to quickly remove a hook by using the string-yank removal technique. This technique is great when you are out fishing and need to remove a hook from the skin quickly. It is also something you don't want to wait to try on yourself until you have to. We'll practice on a pool noodle.

Materials

A HOOK

A PIECE OF POOL NOODLE OR THICK PACKING FOAM

FISHING LINE OR STRING

1. Hook the end of the hook into the pool noodle.

2. Wrap fishing line or string around the mid-point of the bend of the hook.

3. Press the shank (end of the straight part) of the hook against the noodle or foam.

4. Firmly and quickly pull on the line, parallel to the hook point, while continuing to apply pressure to the shank.

HOW TO REMOVE A HOOK

1. Loop fishing line around top of the hook bend.

2. Push down firmly on the shank of the hook.

3. While pushing down on the shank, pull the fishing line up and away.

GET HELP FOR TRICKIER HOOKS

This activity is a great method to remove small hooks from the surface of the skin and other materials. For hooks embedded near your eye, or for hooks that are stuck deep or are large and painful, see a doctor for hook removal. Sometimes you can do more damage by removing bigger hooks, deeper hooks, and hooks near your eyes.

CATCH AND RELEASE

Catch and release is an important part of conservation. Many anglers just enjoy fishing without needing to keep fish. Some waterways are open for fishing, but are entirely catch-and-release only. Even if you are allowed to keep fish in some areas, there will be plenty of times when you will let fish go instead of keeping them. Learning proper catch-and-release techniques will help a fish survive after they have been caught by you.

Materials

THE RIGHT-SIZE ROD, REEL, AND LINE FOR THE SPECIES AND LOCATION YOU ARE FISHING (THIS HELPS QUICKLY REEL FISH IN WITHOUT EXHAUSTING THEM)

BARBLESS HOOKS

NEEDLE-NOSE OR FISHING PLIERS OR FORCEPS

RUBBER LANDING NET (THIS HELPS PROTECT A FISH'S SLIME LAYER AND SCALES)

1. Use barbless hooks or pinch down or "crush" a barb on a hook with pliers.

2. Keep the fish in the water as long as you can.

3. Once a fish is caught, use a rubber net to scoop in the fish.

4. Wet your hands before handling the fish.

5. Never handle fish by grabbing the gills or squeezing the heart.

6. If you want pictures, keep the fish in the water until ready. Quickly lift the fish, snap a photo or two, then return the fish to the water.

7. Use pliers to help remove hooks from fish efficiently and quickly (see safety tip). Pull the hook in the same direction the hook point is embedded in the mouth.

8. Fish have to recover a bit after being caught. Never release a fish before it's ready. To revive a fish, hold it with its head into the current (if in a stream or river) and wait for it to swim off under its own power.

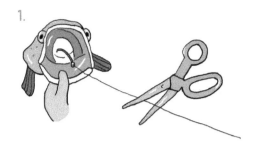

DEALING WITH NERVOUS FISH

Fish can sometimes get nervous and thrash a bit when you try to remove a hook from their mouth. Use pliers or forceps to grab the shank of the hook and carefully remove it. If a fish is thrashing or kicking, let it settle before trying to remove the hook.

KEEP A FISHING LOG

Many of the best anglers in the world keep fishing logs to help them catch more fish. I can't tell you how many times I've gone back to look at pictures and writings to see what I was using to catch fish and where I caught them. Keeping a fishing log will be one of the best tools for you to become a great angler.

Materials

NOTEBOOK OR JOURNAL

PEN OR PENCIL

1 List things that happened on your last fishing trip. Include the date and place where you fished, as well as the bait or lure you used and what you caught.

2 Each time you fish, add to your fishing log. Write about the fun things that happened and who you fished with.

DATE AND TIME : Monday, February 8, 2021; 9:00 a.m.–4:00 p.m.

LOCATION Kenai River, Cooper Landing, Alaska (south shoreline)

WEATHER: Overcast and cold! About 32 degrees and windy.

FISHING WITH: My friends Felix and Jackie and our dogs Max and Gigi

NOTES: I wasn't sure what to expect on this day of fishing. The weather had been really cold for a few weeks, and there was a lot of ice on the water. But it ended up being a lot of fun! We caught two rainbow trout and one Dolly Varden using flesh flies. Gigi jumped out of the boat trying to catch a fish that Jackie caught! It was Gigi's first time on the water, and it turns out she's a great swimmer.

Fish Fact

Seahorses are the only fish that actually swim upright.

DATE AND TIME: ....

LOCATION: ....

....

WEATHER: ....

....

FISHING WITH: ....

....

NOTES: ....

....

....

....

....

....

....

....

....

....

....

....

....

Chapter 5

FRESHWATER FISH

Freshwater fishing is the most popular type of fishing across the United States. Did you know that more than 38 million people fish in fresh water every year? Almost 13 percent of the entire population in the United States fish in fresh water.

This chapter is all about understanding more about the freshwater fish you will catch. You'll learn:

- ☐ **How a fish bladder works**
- ☐ **How fish breathe and see**
- ☐ **What a fish's lateral line is**
- ☐ **How to make dough bait**
- ☐ **How to clean a fish you're keeping**

FLOAT LIKE A FISH

Fish have swim bladders that fill with air or release air depending on the barometric pressure and other things. This activity is a bit of an experiment to see how a fish's swim bladder works. The rise and fall of the bottle depending on how much air is in the balloon is a lot like what happens to fish in water. Their swim bladders are like balloons.

Materials

SMALL GLASS BOTTLE

TUB OR CONTAINER LARGE ENOUGH FOR THE BOTTLE AND DEEP ENOUGH FOR THE BOTTLE TO SINK

WATER

PLASTIC TUBING (12 INCHES OR LONGER)

BALLOON

DUCT TAPE OR OTHER WATERPROOF TAPE

PAPER TOWELS, FOR CLEANUP

1. Fill the tub or container with enough water for the bottle to fully sink.

2. Insert the plastic tube into the balloon and tape the balloon to the tubing with waterproof tape. Make sure the connection is airtight.

3. Place the balloon and part of the tube into the bottle.

4. Tape the tube to the bottle opening.

5. Place the bottle in the water and allow it to sink to the bottom. Keep the other end of the tube out of the water.

6. Blow some air through the tube and into the balloon. What happens to the bottle?

7. Now blow a bit more air into the balloon. Watch the bottle rise.

8. As air releases, you will see the bottle sink again.

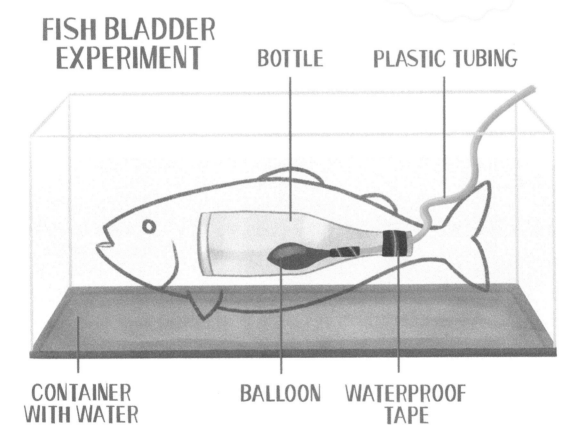

DID YOU KNOW?

The swim bladder helps a fish maintain its position in the water without sinking or floating. The level of air or oxygen adjusts to the fish's surroundings, which keeps it from having to work so hard to stay in the same spot.

FISH BLADDER EXPERIMENT

BOTTLE

PLASTIC TUBING

CONTAINER WITH WATER

BALLOON

WATERPROOF TAPE

BREATHE UNDERWATER

How do fish breathe underwater? If you didn't know, fish have gills that help absorb oxygen from the water. This oxygen is then pumped through the blood by the fish's heart. Carbon dioxide is then released back through the gills and into the water. This activity will illustrate how oxygen particles get filtered out of a fish's gills.

Materials

CLEAR GLASS CONTAINER

CUP

COFFEE FILTER

RUBBER BAND

WATER

1 TABLESPOON COFFEE GROUNDS OR DIRT

1. Cover the top of the glass container with a coffee filter. Wrap the rubber band around the coffee filter so it holds the filter tightly to the glass container.

2. Fill the cup halfway with water.

3. Pour the coffee grounds or dirt into the cup of water.

4. Carefully pour the cup of water onto the filter so the water goes into the glass. Think of the coffee filter as the fish's gills, and the grounds in the water as oxygen. How do gills absorb or "catch" oxygen as a fish swims?

BREATHE LIKE A FISH

RUBBER BAND

WATER

COFFEE GROUNDS

CUP

COFFEE FILTER

GLASS JAR

DO FISH FART?

Though most fish do not fart, strangely enough, herring might actually be guilty of letting out a bit of gas every now and then. Herring use this "fart" to expel air in a fine stream of bubbles. This stream of bubbles makes a high-frequency noise to communicate with other herring.

TALL TAILS

Let's look at how fish use their fins and tails to swim and keep steady in the water. The most powerful fin a fish has is its tail fin, or "caudal" fin. The caudal fin helps a fish propel through the water quickly. It also causes the wavy motion fish are known for.

This activity will help you learn all about various tail shapes and how much water each shape can move. This determines how much power a fish has through the thrust of their tail. A fish might not be the fastest, but with the right kind of caudal fin, they can move lots of water with their tail and have quick bursts of speed.

Materials

STIFF CARDBOARD

SCISSORS

PAPER CUP

1. Cut out various shapes and sizes of different fish fins.

2. Place the paper cup upside down on a smooth table.

3. Using one "fin" at a time, wave your arm and the fin sharply back and forth to try to move the paper cup.

4. Repeat this with each fin. What do you notice? Does the cup slide away quickly, or does it take several tries to move the cup?

DID YOU KNOW?
Parrot fish sleep in a blanket of snot for protection.

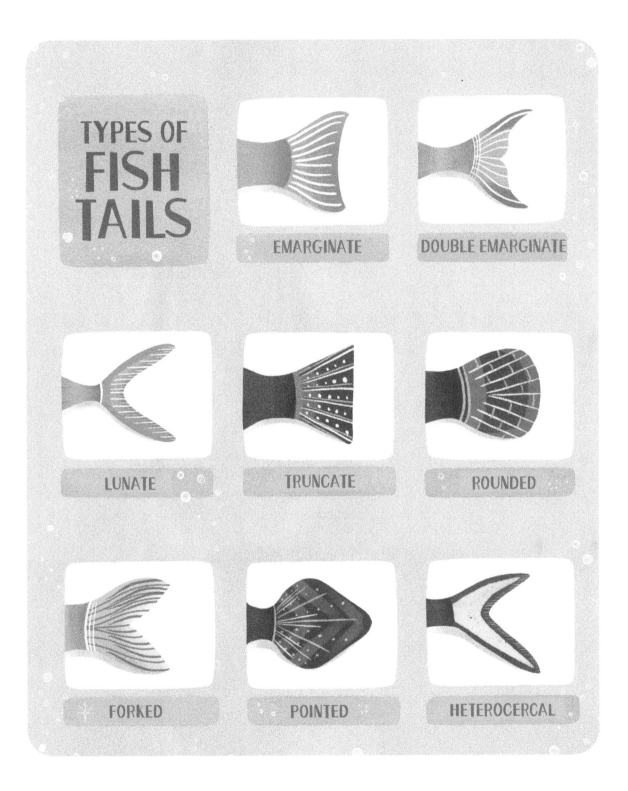

TYPES OF FISH TAILS

EMARGINATE

DOUBLE EMARGINATE

LUNATE

TRUNCATE

ROUNDED

FORKED

POINTED

HETEROCERCAL

SLIMY FISH

Have you ever caught a fish and gotten their slime on you? Fish release a layer of slime through their skin for protection against harmful parasites and diseases. This slime can be thick and smelly, depending on the species, but it is super important for their survival. It's crucial to handle fish carefully so you don't remove their slime. Let's make some fake fish slime to see what it's all about!

Materials

LARGE BOWL

1 TEASPOON BAKING SODA

1 CUP WARM WATER

9-OUNCE BOTTLE ELMER'S LIQUID SCHOOL GLUE

CONTACT LENS SOLUTION

SPOON OR SPATULA

1. In a large bowl, mix the baking soda with the warm water until fully dissolved.

2. Squeeze all the glue into the large bowl.

3. Mix the glue into the warm water mixture until combined.

4. Slowly add the contact lens solution, a little at a time, stirring frequently.

5. Add a little bit of contact lens solution every minute or so until a slime forms. It will become less sticky with a bit more contact lens solution.

BACK IN SCHOOL

Fish use what's called their "lateral line" to help them swim in schools, feel vibrations, sense their prey and wounded food, and stay safe from predators. Their lateral line system also helps keep them oriented in the water and detect pressure changes and currents.

In this activity, you'll get an idea of how a lateral line works. Let's check it out!

Materials

2 TO 4 FEET OF STRING, FISHING LINE, ROPE, OR A STRETCHED-OUT RUBBER BAND

A FRIEND

1. Each person holds an end of the string, fishing line, rope, or rubber band.

2. Pull tightly on both ends.

3. One person closes their eyes.

4. The other person lightly touches the string to see if the person with their eyes closed can detect the touch.

5. Try using various levels of "pressure" on the line to see if you and your friend can feel the movement along the "lateral line."

LATERAL LINE

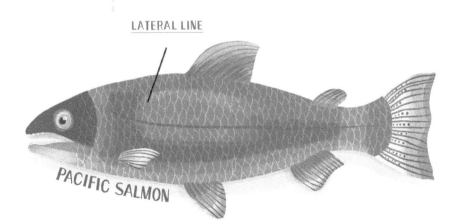

PACIFIC SALMON

FISH-EYE LENS

Ever heard the term "fish eye" or "fish-eye lens"? Well, fish have eyes similar to humans', but they have adapted to help them see underwater. A fish's retina is slightly extended—this is where the term fish-eye lens comes from.

In this activity, we will use an underwater viewer to take a look at what fish see!

Materials

SCISSORS OR KNIFE

CIRCULAR CLEAR PLASTIC CONTAINER WITH A LID (LIKE A DELI-STYLE CONTAINER)

CLEAR PLASTIC WRAP

1. Using scissors or a knife, cut a circle out of the bottom of the container. Do the same to the lid.

2. Stretch a piece of plastic wrap wider than the mouth of the container over the top of the container.

3. Place the lid back on the container.

4. Trim the excess plastic wrap with the scissors.

5. Hold the container against the water so the plastic wrap is against the water. Hold your face to the open end and peek through. You are now getting a fish-eye view!

SAFETY TIP: Have a grownup help with or supervise cutting the plastic container.

MATERIALS

SCISSORS

CONTAINER

RUBBER BANDS

PLASTIC WRAP

UNDERWATER VIEWER

2. Place the plastic wrap over the top of the container and secure with rubber bands. Put the lid over the plastic wrap and cut off the excess.

PLACE THE LID OVER THE PLASTIC

CUT OFF EXCESS PLASTIC WRAP

1. Cut out a hole in the lid and in the bottom of the container.

FILTER FEEDERS

Filter feeders are a class of fish that get their food by filtering out small bits of material and food (like plankton and krill) from the water. Lots of feeder fish (small bait fish) are actually filter feeders, but whale sharks, sockeye salmon, and some herring are also considered filter feeders. In this activity, you'll see how a whale shark uses sieving as a filter-feeding method. Whale sharks have something called dermal denticles attached to their gills. These filter small food particles out of the water as the whale shark swims. The shark sucks in a mouthful of water, closes its mouth, and expels the water through its gills. Any particles larger than 3 millimeters get trapped on the dermal denticles and will be swallowed by the shark. Let's try to mimic filter feeding with an experiment.

Materials

PAPER CUP (PREFERABLY BIODEGRADABLE)

SCISSORS

TESTING TANK, SUCH AS A SINK, FISH TANK, BATHTUB, OR LARGE BOWL

WATER

BAG OF FROZEN PEAS AND CARROTS, THAWED, OR UNCOOKED RICE (FOR "FOOD PARTICLES")

SPOON

SCREEN OR MESH FABRIC

RUBBER BAND

1. Cut off the bottom of the cup.

2. Fill your "tank" with water and add the peas and carrots or rice.

3. Stir the water until the food particles begin to swirl.

4. With your cup with the bottom cut off, try to scoop up as many food particles as you can in 10 seconds. Were you able to catch any food?

5. Since you probably weren't able to catch any food using a cup without a bottom, now try to add some materials to the bottom of the cup to simulate the sieving method of the whale shark.

6. Place the screen or mesh fabric over the bottom of your cup. Secure it with a rubber band.

7. Stir the food particles again.

8. Use your cup with the mesh to catch as much food as you can in 10 seconds. How'd you do? Chances are, you caught lots of food in 10 seconds using the whale shark's sieving method. You can see that whale sharks are very effective filter feeders!

BONUS ACTIVITY

Remove the mesh or screen from the bottom and use other materials like a comb, pipe cleaners, etc. to simulate other filtering methods.

- **Pores:** These are holes that allow water to exit the filter. Only particles smaller than the pore are able to pass through.

- **Cilia:** These are tiny, flexible hairs that collect small food particles and transport them to a collection area.

- **Mucous:** A gooey coating that makes the filter or filter structures sticky, capturing particles it comes into contact with.

- **Combs:** These are rods with ridged, narrow teeth (just like a hair comb) that stick out into the flow of water, trapping particles that are too large to fit between the teeth.

DOUGH BAIT

Because most fish can taste and smell better than humans, they can be attracted to things we may not even detect. However, they can also be attracted to smells that we find quite offensive. If you've ever smelled catfish bait or some of the scents anglers use to attract pacific salmon, you know they can be pretty gross!

In this activity, you will learn how to make a popular dough bait that works great for catfish and carp. Make sure you only use bait where it is legal. Let's dive in!

Materials

MIXING BOWL

1 CUP FLOUR

1 CUP CORNMEAL

1 TEASPOON
GARLIC POWDER

1 TEASPOON SUGAR

1½ CUPS WATER,
DIVIDED

1 CUP MOLASSES

SPOON OR SPATULA

SAUCEPAN

STOVE

SLOTTED SPOON

BAIT DOUGHBALLS

1. In the bowl, mix the flour, cornmeal, garlic powder, and sugar.

2. Add ¾ cup of water to the flour mixture and stir until you get a doughy consistency.

3. Roll the dough into different-size balls, from pea-size to quarter-size.

4. In the saucepan, mix the molasses and the remaining ¾ cup of water and bring to a boil.

5. Once your molasses-and-water mixture is boiling, use the slotted spoon to lower your dough balls into the water.

6. Boil for 3 minutes.

7. Turn off the stove and use the slotted spoon to transfer your dough balls to a tray or plate to dry. Congratulations! You now have your very own fish bait!

SAFETY TIP:
Have a grownup help with and supervise the boiling water and stove use.

DID YOU KNOW?
Pacific salmon can travel very far upstream to their spawning beds. Some salmon have been known to travel up to 2,400 miles to spawn—with no food! What an incredible journey!

HOW TO CLEAN A FISH

We've talked about safe fish handling practices and catch-and-release techniques. There are times, however, when you will want to harvest fish to eat where it is legal. It is important, just like with catch and release, to handle and clean your fish humanely so it won't go to waste. In this activity, we will explore how to clean and fillet a fish you want to keep.

One of the most important things to remember is to keep fish cool and wet until you're ready to eat them. If you're lucky enough to fish in colder water, using a stringer can keep fish fresh for hours. A stringer can be as simple as a piece of rope that you put through the fish's mouth and then out its gill plate before tying the rope into a knot so the fish can't slide off. If you are fishing in warmer water, **live wells** and coolers with ice will keep fish fresh.

Materials

A CLEAN, DRY SURFACE

A FISH YOU'VE CAUGHT OR PURCHASED

A FILLET KNIFE

SAFETY TIP:
Have a grownup help and supervise until you know how to fillet fish.

1. Lay the fish on a clean, dry surface. Cut the fish behind its gills and pectoral fin down to the backbone, being careful not to cut through the backbone.

2. Keeping the knife in the fish, turn the blade and cut through the ribs toward the tail. Use the backbone as a guide.

3. Turn the fish around and finish cutting the meat away from the backbone.

4. Flip the fish and repeat steps 2 through 4.

5. Remove the rib cage and any other small bones in the fish.

6. To remove the skin, place the fish skin-side down. Insert the knife blade ½ inch from the tail. With your other hand, hold the tail firmly and run the blade at an angle between the skin and the meat.

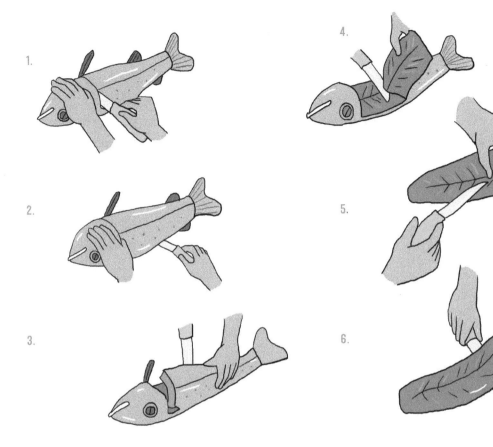

1.

2.

3.

4.

5.

6.

FIELD DRESSING

If you can't fillet a dead fish within a few hours, you'll need to field dress it. This is simply removing the gills, guts, and kidneys, since these will spoil fast in dead fish and make the meat taste bad. To field dress a fish, cut out the red gills, then make a slice down the belly from back to front. With the belly open, remove the intestines and any organs that you see. This will buy you some time until you can fillet the fish properly.

SALT WATER AND FRESH WATER

Did you know there are fish that can live in both fresh water and salt water? These remarkable fish are known as **anadromous** fish. They spend parts of their lives living in fresh water (usually as juveniles) and the rest of their lives as adults in the salt water. They later return to the fresh water to spawn and lay their eggs. Salmon and steelhead are great examples of anadromous fish, especially in the Pacific Ocean. Try this experiment to see what happens when salt water meets fresh water!

Materials

2 CLEAR PLASTIC CONTAINERS THAT CAN BALANCE ON EACH OTHER

WATER

YELLOW AND RED FOOD COLORING

SALT

A THIN, STIFF PIECE OF PAPER, LIKE A CARD

1. Fill both containers up a little bit less than halfway with water.

2. Put a couple drops of yellow food coloring in one container. Put a couple drops of red food coloring in the other container.

3. Put salt in the yellow water (about ½ tablespoon per cup of water). Stir until the salt dissolves.

4. Put the yellow saltwater container in a sink or bathtub.

5. Put the card on top of the red freshwater container.

6. Quickly, but carefully, flip the red freshwater container over onto the yellow saltwater container, while holding the index card on top of the red container to hold the water in. Slide out the index card from between the containers.

What happens? How quickly do the fresh and salt water mix? Why do you think this happens? (Hint: It has something to do with density.) Here's what happens: Though the salt water and fresh water have the same amount of water in them, the salt water also has a lot of salt in it. Because it has more "stuff" in the same amount of space, it is denser than the fresh water. This causes the fresh water to float on top of the salt water for a little while. Eventually, they start mixing together to make brackish (slightly salty) water.

BE A FISHERIES BIOLOGIST

Some people love fish and fishing so much that they dedicate their entire lives to pursuing these wonderful creatures. Some also study them for a living. You could say I'm one of those people. I have dedicated my life to sharing my love for fish and fishing with people from all across the globe as a fishing guide and outfitter in Alaska.

Like me, fisheries biologists are passionate about fish and the environments in which they live. Fisheries biologists play a vital role in understanding fish populations, changes to populations over time, a fish's environment, and what impacts that environment.

These biologists can be responsible for overseeing projects that impact fish and their habitat. They advise others on what will help or hurt fish populations. When you're ready to pick a path in life, being a fisheries biologist is a great way to work with fish every day!

CAST OFF!

Congratulations on working through all 50 of these fun activities! I am so glad you could join me in this fun process of becoming an angler. Fishing has changed my life, and I hope it has an incredible impact on yours!

There will be times when you will feel like the greatest angler on earth and other times when you will be scratching your head wondering how to catch a fish. The ups and downs of fishing are never-ending. They make fishing such a fun, surprising, and exciting pastime. Enjoy the process, and hopefully I will see you out on the water someday!

LIFE LIST

Track some of your most memorable moments, fish you caught, and details about the location where it all happened. This could be your biggest fish, the most fun you had, or a time when you learned something awesome about fishing or yourself.

	DATE	FISH TYPE	LOCATION	MEMORABLE MOMENTS
1.	6/2/21	Bass	Lake Erie	It was huge! 23 inches long
2.	6/4/21	Yellow perch	Lake Erie	My first catch with a spoon lure!
3.				

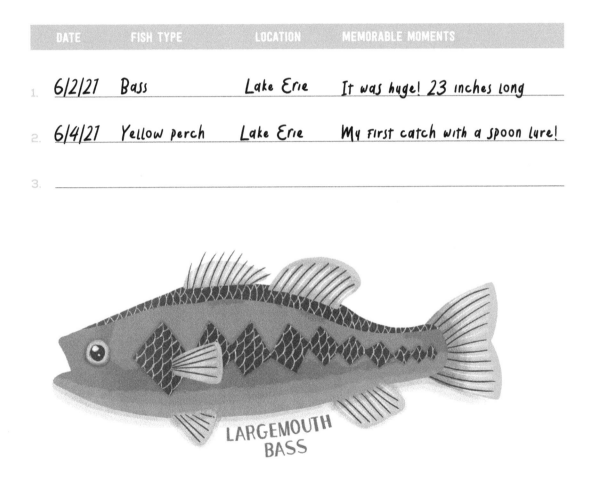

LARGEMOUTH
BASS

DATE	FISH TYPE	LOCATION	MEMORABLE MOMENTS

1. _____

2. _____

3. _____

4. _____

5. _____

6. _____

7. _____

8. _____

9. _____

10. _____

11. _____

12. _____

13. _____

14. _____

15. _____

DATE	FISH TYPE	LOCATION	MEMORABLE MOMENTS

16. _____

17. _____

18. _____

19. _____

20. _____

21. _____

22. _____

23. _____

24. _____

25. _____

26. _____

27. _____

28. _____

29. _____

30. _____

GLOSSARY

action – How much of the rod deflects (bends) when you put pressure on the tip

anadromous – Fish born in fresh water that spend most of their lives in salt water and return to fresh water to spawn

barbless hooks – Hooks without the v-shaped sharp edge that points in a different direction at the end of the hook

barometric pressure – The measurement of air pressure in the atmosphere

bobber – A small float used to suspend bait at a certain depth in the water. Bobbers also let you know if you have a bite or a fish on your hook.

braid – Fishing line composed of several small lines braided together. It's very thin and strong, but tangles easily.

casting – The act of throwing bait or a lure with a fishing line out over the water using a flexible fishing rod

drag – A pair of friction plates inside of fishing reels. If the fish pulls on the line hard enough, the friction is overcome and the reel rotates backward, letting line out and preventing the line from breaking.

fluorocarbon – Thin fishing line that sinks and is virtually invisible to fish in water

leader – Smaller and lighter fishing line tied at the end of the main line

live well – A tank of water on a boat that can be used to store fish you are keeping to eat

lure – Artificial or "fake" fishing bait that is used to attract a fish. Lures use movements, flash, vibrations, and sometimes even scent to attract a fish.

monofilament – The most common type of fishing line, which breaks down easily in water

power – A rod's resistance to bending under a given amount of weight

rig – The equipment at the end of your fishing line that you are using to catch fish

sinkers – Weights used to pull your baited hook to a desired depth

split shot sinkers – small circular metal sinkers that are crimped onto your line with pliers

standing line – The fishing line that is coming off the reel's spool

stringer – A line of rope used to secure your fish and keep them in the water until ready to harvest

structure – The ditches, valleys, and bumps that form the landscape under the water

swivel – A metal gadget that keeps your line from tangling and twisting. It usually has two outer rings and a pivot point in the center.

tackle – Equipment used by anglers when fishing

tag end – The very end of the fishing line you are trying to tie

terminal tackle – Gear that is attached to the end of a fishing line

weights – A common term for sinkers that are used to pull your hook, bait, or fly to a desired depth

RESOURCES

Cooper Landing Fishing Guide's YouTube Channel & Website

CooperLandingGuide.com

Gone Fishing—Logbook for Kids: Observe and Record Your Catches **by David Lisi**

An excellent fishing journal and companion to this book

Keep Fish Wet

For catch-and-release tips; KeepFishWet.org

Take Me Fishing

Comprehensive fishing information; TakeMeFishing.org

Trout Unlimited

Habitat and coldwater fish protection; TU.org

About the Author

David Lisi is a lifelong angler and now owns a fishing guide and outfitter business on the Kenai Peninsula in Alaska. Fishing has always been a part of David's life. Some of his earliest memories are of him fishing in diapers with his family at the lake in upstate New York.

He spent most of his youth exploring the rivers and lakes near his hometown. Eventually, he made his way to Alaska where he now lives and takes people from all around the globe fishing on the world-famous Kenai River for rainbow trout, Dolly Varden trout, and Pacific salmon.

Not a day goes by that he isn't fishing or thinking about fishing!

Printed in the USA
CPSIA information can be obtained
at www.ICGtesting.com
JSHW070214010424
59884JS00002B/7